Against All Odds

By
Diane Upton

Published by Express Book Writing.

www.expressbookwriting.com

Printed in United States of America

Table Of Contents

1) New Beginnings 1

2) The Man In The Trunk 3

3) Life In The Wild 9

4) Baby Steps 12

5) A Reversal Of Fortune 18

6) How To Win A One-Way Trip 23

7) Camping In New Jersey 28

8) Learning The Fun De'mentals. 37

9) Making Friends With Wildlife. 42

10) It's The Little Things That Matter Most 49

11) Motel 6 ¾ 59

12) How To Develop A Healthy Relationship With Your Kidnapper Without Dying. 71

13) The Waffle House 79

14) Enjoying The Open 86

15) Life In An Easybake Oven. 97

16) Outta Control 102

17) Prayer Works In Stange And Wonderful Ways 107

18) Old Acrobats Never Die 112

19) Finding Home 120

1) New Beginnings

It was such a lovely evening for a drive. Myrtle gripped the wheel with her tiny white knuckles and hummed a merry tune. The horns and screaming behind her were just another cacophony of street sounds that Myrtle took as a part of her outing. She was on a mission. Her black/gray hair tied up in a grandmother bun, and loose strands fluttered in the breeze, and with each sharp turn of the wheel, toolboxes, jacks, and tire irons pummeled the man hogtied in her trunk.

Myrtle ran a halfway house and recognized the man when he arrived to rent a room from her old Victorian boarding house. He was fresh from jail, in a cheap suit and sneakers, and standing on her stoop holding the newspaper. His hair slicked down with water he had dipped from her birdbath on his way up the drive, and a weak smile hung on his face like a wet rag over a doorknob. The light that had once shown in his eyes had extinguished and left behind a host of ashes and dead shadows. He was just another soul who had lost himself in the maze of the civilized world.

The State had contacted Myrtle and told her he might arrive. They gave her a copy of his illustrious history of petty robberies and foolishness. So Myrtle stood in her doorway and eyed him up and down and made the decision to let him the room, figuring that maybe her cooking and some time spent doing proper chores under her motherly direction would put some light back into those dead eyes of his; after all, you don't throw someone away just because life has dinged them up a bit; and let's face it, Myrtle had seen and dealt with far worse. Her house was a state-sanctioned halfway house for repeat offenders of controlled substances and petty crimes. They came, stayed, got themselves back together, or they didn't, but they were all welcomed to give life another shot through Myrtle's misfit emporium.

Myrtle ran a tight ship; she gave them good hot meals and chores with a lesson from time to time and had seen many of her former occupants find their way back into society. It was a good gig, albeit tough, but Myrtle was up to the challenge. She had five rough-and-tumble brothers and three sisters, which aided significantly in developing Myrtle's survival skills and she applied her skills in helping to reform the un-reformable. Myrtle believed that every soul was unique, and some souls just needed a little kickstart, and this is how she felt about the man who was now the one kicking and screaming in her trunk.

2) The Man In The Trunk

The man in the trunk had a difficult childhood, born to acrobats who worked in a traveling circus. His mother weaned him on elephant trough water and stale popped corn, and his father once glued his feet to the back of the elephant, telling Harbal that he could stand up and ride the Elephant without falling off and that the stunt would make for great showmanship. Unfortunately, the elephant bolted out the tent door when the glue got hot, leaving the boy embedded in the Big Top canvas. Everyone laughed as they peeled him off the canvas wall, especially his father, who found the incident so entertaining that he approached the Ring Master about including it in an act. The Ring Master, an idiot in Harbal's father's eyes, had turned him down, citing that the insurance company would refuse to pay for repairs to the tent, and walked away shaking his head at Harbal's father. Harbal's exposure to education had been brief and struggling, but by the time he reached twelve years old, he could spell his name in the snow with the precision of a neurosurgeon; what more does a young man need to know?

Harbal's childhood was not completely gloomy; he had a guardian angel. She had also been an acrobat working for another traveling circus. When the two circuses crossed paths, she always came to see Harbal. The first time she came, they were both about six years old. She would find him wherever he slept in the straw near the elephant pen, box car, or under a carriage, and sit beside him in the darkness, silently placing her small, callused hand on his. He figured he was the only other person of her age that she knew. She seldom spoke. But her gentle hand on his was all the dialog he needed. For Harbal, this was the only kind human contact he had ever experienced. She would often sit holding his hand in silence until he fell asleep, then she would be gone. Sometimes, when she came, she brought sweets that she would share with him, another rare treat for Harbal, and sometimes, she would leave a few coins or a wooden toy. But she never stayed and never varied from her routine. She had pretty much haunted (but in a good way) Harbal's childhood.

Once, an opportunity came for Harbal to use the coins she left him to buy a ticket to her flying Circus and attend her family's performance. He discovered her name was Joanna Concello. She wasn't beautiful, not even in her tiny tight outfit with feathers in her hair, but she had a pure heart, grace, and style and could fly like a bird. She did not see him, one small face in a sea of hundreds below, but Harbal watched her with rapt attention as she fluttered like a butterfly in the thin air above the audience. She must be an angel, he thought to himself. Harbal understood the skill to appear weightless and confident while hurtling toward a tiny target like someone's hands.

Harbal admired her courage because his parents were high-wire performers also. His mother trained him as a high wire "catcher" when he was ten. His early indoctrination into the world of spotlights and gasping crowds became necessary as a stand-in for his father, who was often too drunk to find the tent, let alone catch his mother mid-air forty feet above the ground. So, at the tender age of ten, his mother began training him as a high-wire catcher, and like all high-wire performers, his mother taught Harbal to think of the audience as alligators: it made the tricks more fun and reduced the stress that comes from thousands of eyeballs focused on one small moving point which is YOU. He started "catching" regularly after his father failed to appear for the job time after time. His first experience in front of an audience was the day his father and two monkeys, dead drunk, had passed out in their cage, and Daddy did not show up for the evening performance. Harbal's mother retrieved Harbal, asleep in a pile of bunting, jammed some sequined tights on him, and shoved him, terrified, into the arena for his first public appearance as a catcher.

At ten years old, Harbal was a small boy, and when he swung out from the platform for the first time in the position of the catcher, the entire tent went silent. Harbal, terrified, took that silence as a bad sign, sensing their fear and disapproval. His mother, on the opposite side of the rigging in her tight turquoise leotard, gripped the swing in one hand, looking out across the still and deathly silent audience with absolute determination, and graciously extended her other hand toward Harbal as a means of introduction. The audience remained silent instead of the usual applause as she dropped her arm, grabbed the swing in both hands, and left the landing in a courageous leap. In mid-air, forty feet above the ground and flying thirty MPH, she performed two summersaults and a back flip above Harbal and descended from the sky at about forty MPH toward the platform, where Harbal then swung out toward her, hanging by his legs. Their hands connected. He caught her dead on, using his momentum to swing her back up into the air with a liquid motion, which she used to perform one more summersault, and dropped back toward Harbal as his swing brought him up to meet her. Their hands connected, and he swung them back to the landing, caught the rail, and landed them simultaneously on the pad. The audience went wild, along with the entire circus company, who were also holding their breath that his mother would not end up as a large red stain on the floor of the Big Top. His mother stepped forward and took a bow to the roaring audience below, and Harbal, stepping back, watching her take that bow. just like the audience, Harbal was in awe of his mother's amazing flying skills.

As the years went by, Harbal's head-liner father forbade Harbal's name from appearing in the playbill, although Harbal had continued standing in for his besotted patriarch for years. During the day, while Harbal set pegs, fed elephants, and carried bunting, he was uncomfortably aware of the other performers watching him from the corners of their eyes. It gave him a creepy sensation and left him feeling threatened and isolated. He grew to believe he was not welcome as a usurper of his father's job.

Then his life in the shadows of his headliner father ended abruptly the day his parents died in a freak accident in the circus. They were eating their lunch on a pedestal on the floor of the Big Top when the same Elephant to whom they had glued their son's feet found an opportunity to sit down on them both. It took some time to convince the elephant to stand back up, and when he did, he displayed what looked like the tattoo of two perfectly flat, screaming people on his backside. The Ringmaster had them scrubbed off with stiff brushes and gave the elephant a quart of peanut Schnapps to dull the pain, along with a subtle nod.

This incident had made Harbal an orphan. He stood watching that drunken Elephant stumble about as what was left of his parents was hosed off the circus floor without so much as a moment of silence. This finalized his decision to run away from the Circus and join the outside world. So, he quickly and quietly gathered his meager belongings and slipped out under the side flap of the Big Top.

Once Harbal left the Circus, his dye was cast on the hard streets of civilized society. Decisions were much harder to make when there were more of them in some regards and almost no choices in other regards. The mean streets did not offer Harbal many good choices. In his constant state in survival mode, he often dreamt of his little girl, who used to come to visit him; she was the only safe, peaceful, and solid thing he knew, and she haunted his sleep, especially when he was in trouble. Harbal missed her very much, and the memory of her small hand in his brought him comfort and grounding even in the hardest of times. But after a while, the dreams of her changed with his circumstances, and he became her 'catcher,' each time her tiny hands reached out to him in mid-air.... she would vanish, leaving an empty swing and a hollow feeling in the pit of his stomach. Harbal knew that that phase of his life was over, so he shut out those pointless dreams and moved on.

3) Life In The Wild

Harbal was unprepared for what he found in the civilian world. The skulduggery of civilized society was much the same as in the three-ring Circus. He encountered the same sideward glances, disdain, and danger he had suffered for sixteen years. In addition, there was no justice because the people performing the skulduggery were also in charge of eliminating the skulduggery; and, unlike the Circus where everyone did everything from nursing the sick to performing, he found the deck stacked against him here in polite society. It appeared that all he was fit for was hard manual labor among men who hated him worse than the performers he had left behind. Harbal felt just as isolated and just as unwelcome as he had before. The world was a cold, mean place. The futility of it all eventually forced Harbal into a life of crime.

He was unsuccessful at this venture as well because he had the one thing no self-respecting crook could tolerate: a conscience. Somewhere deep inside of him, he kept this conscience thing well hidden, but now and then, it would rear its inconvenient head.

Once, after swiping an ornate silk coin purse from a cafe' table, he made it less than one block when he heard a young girl wailing over the theft. His feet stopped themselves, making him stand and listen to the sobbing as the waiter admonished the poor girl. His feet then turned him around and took him back to the table, where he presented the purse to a lovely young girl with tears in her eyes. He opened the purse, dropped in all his own meager coins, handed her the fat purse, and ran. He was later apprehended by the local constabulary, who gave him free room and board for the next day until the same young girl came to the station, paid his bail with his own money, and had him released. It was a humiliating experience for an up-and-coming purse snatcher.

Harbal vanished into the cityscape, not to surface again for a year or so. He pumped gas, painted fences, and emptied the glovebox of every car he washed. He became well known to the local boys-in-blue and wore out his light-fingered welcome nearly everywhere he went. After another stretch in the County lock-up, he would be released back into polite society, where he would once again welcome more arrests, a few beatings, and a serious warning from the Mob who strung him up by his feet and beat him with frozen Pepperoni sticks, for cleaning out on of THEIR glovebox's full of hundred-dollar bills. Of all Harbal's correctional experiences, the mob made the greatest impression. Harbal was still a young man, but he was no longer a callow youth and had now lost much of his initial enthusiasm for life free of Ring Masters and glaring roadies. Harbal's joints hurt from his early years in the Circus and the back-breaking work on the ground crew. Everything else, including his spirit, ached from years of neglect and sleeping alone under bridges. So, after the Mob explained his faulty life choices by beating him black and blue, he moved out of the city as far away from the Mob as he could manage and tried robbing convenience stores on the outskirts of town.

With this choice came more head wounds and more time as a guest of the state. Meanwhile, the state was growing tired of his recidivism and decided that Harbal was a candidate for rehabilitation. Harbal's last incarceration provided him with a temporary stipend for rent, a list of halfway houses in the area, and a job with an automobile parts store. So, with his stipend, he was set for about eight weeks with a job training program to teach him a trade. If he passed the training with the auto parts store, he would get another small stipend to hold him over until he could stand on his own two feet. With all this training and rehabilitation, he would be on his way to a fabulous life of skilled labor and civilized poverty... as opposed to the abject poverty that came from doing nothing. His early life in a circus had trained him to work from sunup to sundown, so this little gig went quickly, and once he had earned enough money from the rehabilitation program, he took the advice of his parole officer. He sought refuge in a boarding house outside of Philadelphia. It was a large old Victorian house on a large, wooded lot owned and run by a woman named Myrtle. She had rooms to let at fair prices, served decent food, and was licensed by the State as a facility for reentering society.

4) Baby Steps

Harbal arrived on the doorstep of the boarding house with a folded newspaper in his hands. He had circled the room for let section and was carrying his suitcase and a book titled The Art of the Deal, which he had fished out of a dumpster to use as a prop to make a good impression. A woman named Myrtle answered the door in a loose Muumuu house dress of big bright flowers on a pink background. Her gray-streaked black hair pulled up in a bun that missed half the follicles. The missed follicles were sticking out at odd angles as though, had they not been firmly held at one end, they would have fled for their lives. She had a cigarette hanging from her mouth. She looked for all the world like a smoking Hydrangea bush. She stood in the doorway, staring at Harbal. The smoke from her cigarette curled up in front of one squinted eye as she looked Harbal up and down. "What's your current name?" She asked.

Harbal put on what he thought was a sincere face and said, "Harbal Persons, ma'am, and what's your name?" The smoking Muumuu leaned forward and said, “My name is Ms. Myrtle, and that's all you need to know.” “You here about the room?" she added.

"Yes, ma'am," Harbal replied, sucking in his gut. Her piercing black eyes ran up and down him like a caustic paint stripper, taking in every detail of his person, his shabby suit, worn-down heels, and slicked back hair. She stuck out her hand and said,

"Show me the money." Harbal handed her twenty dollars and said,

"Show me the room." The woman crumpled the money up in her hand and shoved it deep into her pocket; she turned and walked toward the inside of the house. Harbal followed, carefully casing the knickknacks, old china, and dusty bookshelves for anything of value that she might not miss. They climbed the creaking stairs to the third floor. The smoldering Hydrangea bush led him to the end of the hall, where a door stood open. It was a pleasant room, not huge, but it had room for a double bed, a reading chair, a lamp, and a desk. It even had a small TV set on a stand in the corner. The windows were open, and a cool breeze wafted through the room, carrying the slightest hint of Lilacs. Harbal handed her another 20 dollars, which she snapped out of his fingers and stuffed into her pocket to join the twenty he had handed her on the stoop. Then, with one more hard stare at him, she turned and left the room, closing the door behind her.

Harbal smiled crookedly to himself, looking around the room. There was a small TV, and Fresh flowered wallpaper lined the walls with creamy white door and window frames. The hardwood floor, darkened with age, were of wide planks scrubbed clean and shiny. Imagine being in a room with a bed and no bars, he thought to himself as he tossed his suitcase on the bed and snapped the latches open. He removed his crowbar, hacksaw, and wire cutters and shoved them under the bed. He struck something. So, he got down on his hands and knees and fished out a heavy shoe box, opened the box lid, and jumped. The shoe box was full of bones. Harbal caught his breath and sat down on the floor.

A muffled voice came through the door behind him, saying,

"THAT's so's you know not to mess with me. Dinner is at 6PM sharp. If you ain't there at 6PM sharp, you get no meal."

He heard her loose slippers slapping and squeaking along the corridor and down the hall out of earshot. Harbal sighed. He had seen worse and survived worse. He decided that he would do well here. He closed the shoebox and shoved it back under the bed beside his tools. He was going to feel right at home. The landlady, although as mean as a boil, had implied that she would say nothing of his activities if he ate and paid the rent on time. It was not that much different from the Circus he grew up in, or the jails he had known. People were constantly barking orders, others passing through, sharing mealtimes, and avoiding the Warden or the Ring Master and his nasty little carriage whip. Harbal decided that he would like to try living indoors for a change and he would get to like this.

The thing about luxury and comfort is that when those two commodes are satisfied the extra energy they free opens up other opportunities. Remember the adage of an idle mind is the Devils workshop, and Harbal had a penchant for making bad decisions. For example, once when Harbal had collected enough money to eat and rent a motel room, he felt he was moving up in his profession and filled with this bravado, he tried to rob a fireworks store. After casing the store and establishing that the owner was unarmed, the store was closed at 9PM and the owner gone, Harbal returned to the business in the dead of night, broke a side window, and was immediately shot with a Chinese bottle rocket that put a crease in the top of his head that he had to comb over. Harbal had not considered that the owner of the establishment also lived there or that fireworks were not that much different than guns.

Harbal was settling into his new routine in the warm bosom of Myrtle's halfway house, with days of regular meals, chores, and legitimate employment rolled past like snapshots in someone else's album. Harbal's body and frame filled out to its proper twenty-eight-year-old portions with all that decent food, and the routine at the house and his job, gave him structure. The old lady was a good cook, and the dining room was always packed for these meals. Myrtle never turned anyone away hungry. People ate quietly, minding their own business, which you can be sure was best left undisclosed.

The landlady was good to her word. She kept the house clean, the linens washed, and the bathrooms scrubbed spotless. It was a good place. The other boarders came and went with regularity. Sometimes they went out a window, but the Landlady was always magically waiting for them. Harbal found it hilarious each time this aging muumuu cigarette-smoking woman miraculously hoisted one of those scrawny escapees up by his feet and shook until the rent fell out. He noticed she was not as old or overweight as he had first thought. She still had a lot of fight left in her. So Harbal kept his head down, he had seen enough to know that she was generous but not stupid. He paid his rent on time, ate his meals promptly at 6 PM, and turned his small TV off at 11 PM.

Harbal Persons was becoming a regular member of society, and as he gained a little stability, his organized time allowed him to revisit his old memories. He began to think about his past, and all his thoughts and memories would culminate at one spot, his little friend who used to visit him and hold his hand in his darkness. Remembering the feel of that small act of kindness, was the only real connection holding him to the planet. It was safe to think about her once again after all these years and Harbal began to wonder how she was doing, but reality has a way of slipping in sharp edges to his memories and it would all end in the abysmal pit of reality. Harbal was a grown man, and miles and years away from that life. His old life had been fraught with doubts, hunger, danger, and loneliness, and conversely, this new life came with the same things but in different forms. The memory of her quiet kindness in the maelstrom of his young life was no longer sufficient to quell the storm, and thoughts of the peace her tiny hand had once given him were gone for ever.

5) A Reversal Of Fortune

After a few months of steady work and no jails Harbal began to grow up, but not quite as quickly as he puffed up. He decided that since he was gainfully employed and obviously successful, he should start his own business. It did not look so hard, all you had to do was buy things to sell. He could still be his own man, make his own way in the world. He would be important. Harbal began to pay much closer attention to his job in an automobile parts department of a dealership, how inventory was purchased, organized, and cost. He wrote down the names of the suppliers and named his new company "Harbal Hazit" This idea of being his own boss would make him rich and important, so armed with all the information he could find he acquired a few auto parts and began selling them from the back door of the dealership. After all, he needed seed money for his venture and 'acquiring' was half the deal.

However, His boss did not appreciate or understand this new enterprise of Harbals the day he came in through the back door to retrieve his coat, and found a line of people, cash in hand, walking away with items he recognized. When the yelling stopped, Harbal found himself once again unemployed in the dustbin of society. But he still considered his enterprise mildly successful by keeping the purloined funds and not being re-housed by the State. His ex-boss was a kind man. But now, without income, Harbal knew his room at

Myrtle's dead-end emporium was gone at the end of the month. The heat was on, and having grown accustomed to the luxury of a bed, and regular meals Harbal had to find some way to maintain his new lifestyle. He would have to lie like a rug for the next thirty days to keep his landlady from turning him into a box of bones under someone else's bed...and so, the saga of Harbal began...

Harbal rose every morning, dressed, grabbed a coffee in the kitchen where Mable always kept a fresh pot on the burner and left the house. He had to keep up appearances for the landlady while he tried to find another employer dumb enough to hire him. Each afternoon at the end of a hard morning of finding out all the things he was unqualified to do, Harbal walked to the nearest park and sat under a tree to watch the squirrels steal peoples lunch bags. With the sun well past the high noon mark he would climb to his feet and walk back to the Boarding house. Dinner at 6PM. Harbal sat at the table head down minding his own business and figuring that every night could be his last good meal. After all the Landlady was only tolerable if you followed the rules, and not paying the rent was one of those rules.

This situation was forcing Harbal back into his normal bad habits, which were hazardous at the best of times. Either he would have to pack up and find a nice bridge to sleep under or come up with a new scheme to get his hands on enough money to tied him over. Convenience stores were out, they all knew him on sight, there wasn't a church within twenty miles of where he sat, that would let him near a poor box, even though he qualified. Car washes were out for the same reason as convenience stores, and it was cleaning out the wrong glove box that got him introduced to the Mob, he worried about that because the Mob was everywhere.

Harbal being Harbal, could not take money from children either, but old ladies in big, flowered Muumuus were another thing. Harbal hatched an idea. What if Myrtle kept money stashed around the house the same way she stashed bones. He chuckled at the thought of paying his rent with Myrtles own money. Harbal sat quietly in his room that night hatching a master plan. He figured he had been caught thieving because he did not think things through. But not this time; this time, he would cover all his bases before finding where she stashed rent money. Harbal had never seen the old woman leave the property. Groceries and Gin were delivered, and she mostly took care of maintenance by herself, or would assign borders simple jobs. She had arranged tasks for them like raking leaves, painting, plumbing repairs and managed to teach them enough to get them interested in a trade. Doing repairs for her garnered rewards like one week off the rent, or homemade pastries. The old lady was a good cook.

So Harbal hatched a plan to help her with maintenance around the property while he searched the house to find where she hid the weekly income. With pencil and paper in hand he did the math, twelve rooms, forty dollars a week. She only took cash, and she never left the property. So, the money had to be here, and if he could find that stash, she would not notice a few greenbacks missing from that pile and he could continue to enjoy the luxury of a room, bed, TV and hot meals. Myrtle agreed to his request of assignments and gave him tasks in exchange for breakfast added to his meals. His first job was to vacuum carpets, wash dishes and pull weeds. With his new assignment Harbal began walking casually around the house, looking at books on their community shelf, opening bottom draws of hutches, and outside under the bushes. He walked the stairs, pressing here and there and stopping when someone looked his way, he would turn on his vacuum cleaner and push it quickly back and forth. He would wait for Myrtle or the other tenants to walk down a hall, and if there were squeaky boards, he would dash over to that spot and make a note of its location on a pad he kept. Later at night while everyone was settling in, he would go back and check the squeaky boards to see if they were completely loose with anything hidden beneath.

He was developing a detailed plan using his combined organizational skills learned by sorting car parts and his vast experience with breaking and entering. But it had become apparent that Myrtle's larder was not hidden under the floorboards, or in the bookcases. So, he was forced to advance his plan to enter her private area of the house. He considered anything that might give him away once he was ready to tackle her area. He drew up charts to mark where the boards squeaked and oiled his bedroom door hinges while other lodgers stared at him like he was a camel in a dress. He would smile and say Myrtle had assigned him this chore. He measured the distance from his door to Myrtle's room on the first floor and back out through the front door. Moving outside, he searched several outbuildings for places to hide right under her nose if she got a whiff of his master plan. He also paced the distance from the front door to the nearest bus stop to plan his escape route and added a bus schedule to his growing pile of reconnaissance materials.

He studied his plan out of sight in his room every night. Myrtle's rooms on the first floor were slightly over from his upstairs window, he knew she drank Gin and would sleep soundly, so he watched her lights and knew when she was asleep. He made a note of her schedule. Then he would turn in for the night.

6) How To Win A One-Way Trip

Now Myrtle had been in the halfway house business for a number of years since her husband died. She was about as naive as a zookeeper. She knew what 'casing a joint' looked like. Sweetening the plot, the State had informed her that Harbal was once again unemployed. This validated her suspicions about his note taking. So, whenever Harbal made a note of a squeak, Myrtle made a note of it as well. She had a notebook of her own, where she documented his schedule and would watch Harbal's bedroom light from her downstairs window, and when it went out, she would grab her flat pry bar and start at the base of the stairs, gently loosening different boards. In the morning, she would hear Harbal cursing under his breath for finding more squeaky places on the stairs and landings than had been there the day before. When Harbal left for 'work,' she would then hammer down the original squeaky boards so they would be silent. After Harbal would come home from 'work' and go to his room, practicing stepping around all the squeaks he had documented that morning, he would find them gone, and everywhere else he stepped, it squeaked.

This stair squeak game consumed them both. Harbal, with frustration, was trying for all he was worth to find any squeak that would give him away, while Myrtle, in exuberance, was right behind him, changing every single one and having the time of her life. Finally, Harbal began stomping about the landings and steps in confused rage. "Stomp, stomp, squeak, squeak, squeak Step, squeak, stomp, stomp, stomp. His mutterings became rants against nature, God, and the migrating nature of squeaks. Myrtle, relaxing in her TV chair, just sipped her gin and tonic and laughed.

As time passed the days of faking his employment and casing the house were drawing to an end as his money ran out. It was time to set the wheels of his plan into motion to secure his residential future. He waited quietly in his room after dinner until it was late, and Myrtle's light was turned off. He was going to play it smart, and finding the stash, he would only take one month's rent at a time; she'd never miss it, and he could keep this gig going indefinitely. The time had come. Harbal opened his liberally oiled door very quietly; he stepped out of his room into the hall, carefully identifying all the safe spots he had cataloged in his journal.

The floor squeaked where he had carefully stepped. He froze. He took another cautious step...SQUEAK. He stopped dead. He pulled out his notebook and rechecked the squeak chart. Repositioning himself, he took another step. Silence, and another. Silence. He smiled confidently and began descending the stairs to the second floor. SQUEAK SQUEAK SQUEAK SQUEAK, he threw himself against the wall on the stairs. Beads of sweat were forming on his forehead. He waited there long enough to make sure no one had heard him.

It was 2 AM, and all the other boarders were fast asleep. He moved carefully down the stairs to the second floor, squeaking past another four rooms, a bath, and a broom closet. As he descended the stairs to the first floor, the wooden treads sang out in a cacophony of squeaks that culminated in the last board flipping off the stairs altogether and clattering loudly to the bare wooden floor taking Harbal with it. He lay there face down on the worn carpet cringing.

What would he tell her if she came out of her quarters and asked him why he was face down on her sitting room floor? He waited for her door to open, but nothing happened. After a few moments passed and he was not staring at her fluffy pink bedroom slippers, he sighed in relief and climbed to his feet and got down to business. He quietly searched the small bookcase filled with knickknacks, Myrtle's desk, and the table beside her TV chair. Nothing. He heard her cough in her room. He froze in place and waited. He noticed many empty bottles of gin lined up by the basement door and knew she was a sound sleeper. So, he continued to search the chest where her TV sat, the sofa cushions, and the chair seat. Still nothing. Maybe he could just smother her in her sleep and run the boarding house himself; no one would miss her. He surprised himself that he even thought that way. Harbal was not as ruthless as his lifestyle required. He dismissed this thought as he stood in front of her bedroom door. Every fiber in his body knew the money was in that room, and likely under the bed where she was snoring.

He stood there for another moment, letting the dread and trepidation drain away enough to embark on the last phase of his search. Silently slipping into her bedroom, he got low on the floor below the edge of her mattress. She was loudly snoring face down on her bed, wrapped in blankets. Harbal lay down on the floor and crawled closer to her bed. Retrieving a small LED flashlight from his shirt pocket, he peered underneath Myrtle's bed for shoe boxes, and there they were. BINGO, he had found the mother-load.

He swallowed and tried to slow his breathing, then quietly slid one box out from under the bed frame and opened it, filled with twenty-dollar bills. His frugal plan to take only what he needed for the rent week after week evaporated like spit on a hot griddle. His heart rate pounded in his ears. He stuffed the bills in his pant pockets, fighting down his excitement; he stuffed the bills down his shirt, then slid the box back under her bed and pulled out another one. It, too, was filled with twenties. This was more money than he had ever seen at one time. He pulled out another shoe box and another; he was lost in his ecstasy when suddenly a tiny but firm hand gripped his hair and pulled his head up. What he saw next in the warm, friendly glow of the nightlight on the wall beside him was a fist the size of a walnut with the speed of a locomotive growing larger in his vision. Then he saw the lights blinking in his head, and everything went black.

Harbal woke with a headache. He had no idea where he was until he felt the car's movement and the gravel crunching under the tires. He was in the trunk of a car. The trunk was utterly dark, but as his eyes adjusted, he could make out a coil of rope, toolboxes, tire irons, jacks, and a full gas can. He was wrapped with duct tape over his hands, feet, and mouth. As he inventoried the objects in his immediate surroundings, it occurred to him that he had gone from a stealthy second-story man to a duct-taped imbecile in the trunk of a car, alone with a rope and a gas can. Harbal knew without a shadow of a doubt that Myrtle was with the mob; he had robbed a Maw, probably some gangster's giddy old aunty.

7) Camping In New Jersey

Harbal panicked and began kicking the trunk lid, making his captor, whoever it was, aware that he was awake and done with this nonsense. But each time he kicked the lid of the trunk, the car would veer right or left, and Harbal came into uncomfortable contact with the tumbling jack and the sailing tire iron, which left their mark on his face. After an hour in the dark trunk, he could not tell up from down, and after two hours, he was black and blue. He had no idea what the driver was up to, where he was being taken, or how in hell he had come to find himself in this position in the first place, a big, strong guy like him. Another hour went by. Harbal was thirsty and had to pee. He tried kicking the trunk lid again, but that resulted in several sharp turns involving gas cans, wrenches, and something that smelled like a bag of old tuna sandwiches pummeling his face in the darkness. Another three hours passed; Harbal was now lying humiliated in a cold, wet puddle in the darkness of the trunk and covered with bruises. After expressing his anger again for the umpteenth time against the trunk lid and getting the same result, the anger period passed, and his head cleared; that was when he fully remembered the heist. He remembered the tiny hand yanking back his head and the fist. He had been caught red-handed in a robbery. He was suddenly far more concerned about why he was in the trunk of a car, with his hands and mouth duct taped, instead of in police custody and a jail cell with other extraordinarily stupid people like himself. The change in this standard protocol was disturbing and further supported his abject fear that he had robbed the wrong person. He cringed as he remembered the frozen pepperoni sticks and the pizza the Mob had made once they thawed and had eaten in front of him as he swung upside down on a chain.

The car, now on rough ground, came to a halt. He could hear feet on the sand. Someone was walking down the side of the car. The trunk lid opened, and Harbal flinched and squinted in the weak evening light. A shadow fell across him, and a voice said:

"We're camping here."

Harbal, now peering over the edge of the trunk, knew precisely where 'here' was; fear jolted down his spine. They were in the New Jersey Pine Barrons, home to the Jersey Devil and also known as the Mafia Burial Grounds. The flowered Muumuu reached into the trunk and, grabbed his shirt and belt in both of her hands and heaved him up over the side of the trunk like he weighed no more than a bag of wine corks. She dropped him to the ground beside the trunk. Harbal thought of the rope and the gas can again and held his breath, eyes as wide as bus windows. The Muumuu casually walked about, picking up kindling and using her foot to push the sand and form a fire ring. She lit the fire and pulled up a section of wood for a seat. She lit a cigarette and sat for a few minutes sizing up the heap of grizzled stupidity on the ground by the trunk. Then she stood up and unloaded her tent and sleeping bag from the back seat of her car and set up her gear. Stretching, she opened a can of Pepsi and sat back down on the log. Harbal heard himself whimper involuntarily.

"You missed dinner," she said. "It was 6 PM an hour ago, and you weren't there. Those are the rules."

Harbal had not noticed that he was hungry. He was all too aware of his thirst. He kept watching her down the Pepsi, her throat working, beads of condensation rolling down the side of the cold can. When she finished, she crumpled the can and stood up, grabbed a bottle of water while walking toward where he lay in the sand.

"You are truly one insufferable asshole, son." she muttered, "and we are here to put an end to that," She added as she approached him. Reaching her hand deep into her pocket, she pulled out a stiletto. Harbal winced. She flicked the deadly weapon open, tossed it expertly upside down, and caught it in lightening quick fingers. She stopped in front of him with the gleaming weapon gripped in her fist.

"Don't move, "I ain't responsible for you losing your lips, nose, or one of your eyes if you move,"

She glared down at him. He held as still as his trembling body would allow as he watched the point of that knife swing sideways toward his face, sunlight glittering off the blade as it sank directly between his lips, slicing a perfect hole in the duct tape for her to slip through a straw. She gave him a drink. The cool water washed down his throat, filling him with life again, like a desert after a storm. He felt better. He looked up at the woman who stood over him, still holding the knife.

"From now on," she said, "I will be your guide on this coming tour.

Now, like I told you before, don't give me no sass, and I won't give you no scars."

She stepped away from him and walked back to the car; reaching through the window into the back seat, she pulled out a blue tarp, shook it open, and dropped it over Harbal, covering him from head to foot. She wished him a good night, then turned on her heel and walked to her tent, where she crawled through the flap and was silent.

Generally speaking, NJ has no large dangerous wildlife, but that does not mean it is devoid of charm. New Jersey has the largest mosquito population this side of Alaska. Harbal, now lying under the tarp as the fading blue light washed over him, was comfortable on the ground where he had always slept. Still, he was getting very stiff from being taped together, and he figured that the older woman was mad to think he would not escape into these woods. She'd never find him. So, Harbal waited until he heard her snoring begin, and using his head, legs, and elbows, he began to back crawl out from under the tarp and away from her camp toward the forest. Inch by inch, he put distance between himself and that crazy Muumuu- woman- thing. Inch by inch, he crawled toward a low-lying area hidden from her view. Yes, he would crawl down into the depression, work his bonds loose, and be away from her by morning. He was happy to forget the shoe boxes full of money and the life of luxury that came with all those greenbacks, and he just wanted to stay alive and away from this situation. So, he worked his way down into the hollow, where he could not be easily spotted. And as the night descended and the crickets chirped and sang love songs to one another, he began his great escape.

There was a small puddle of standing water in the bottom of the hollow where he was twisting and turning the tape on his wrists, and this tiny puddle was home to many of the local mosquitos—moms, dads, aunts,' uncles, little brothers and sisters, and many cousins. Harbal, much to his dismay, had delivered them a cookout. Within minutes of trying to work his bonds loose, he heard the buzzing and felt their soft, delicate touch. Within a few more minutes, the happy little mosquitos went to work and found all of Harbal's major and minor veins and arteries. The little cousins found his flesh between the veins and arteries, and some distant relations found the rest. They were all lined up along his blood buffet line with little plates and forks, and they dipped into his blood supply repeatedly. Harbal was squirming and thrashing like he was set on fire. If he flipped himself over, they'd bite his back; if he rolled around, they just hung on. These were good ol' down-home party mosquitoes, and they did not often get dinner and a show like this one. Soon, more were coming from the surrounding puddles where they had received telegrams about the great squirming feast taking place in the puddle up the woods. The air was a blackened swarm descending over Harbal. Some were so large that they lumbered more than they flew; Harbal could feel them land and then dig in. They seemed to like his face the best.

Despite his kicking and squirming, the feast continued until daybreak; the ground was littered with little unconscious bodies of those over-indulgers who had drunk themselves into comas. The rest had returned home to their respective puddles. Harbal could not open his eyes; he could not move his nose or mouth because they were swollen shut. But as he lay there, nearly whimpering in exhaustion and itching like mange, he became aware of someone standing over him. He could hear Myrtle brushing her teeth. She spat to the side and said,

"I took you for a smarter man than you appear to be."

Harbal froze when he heard the zing of the stiletto again and winced for the blow, when he felt her cut through his bindings. Relief flooded his arms and legs when he could move them again. He still couldn't see very well, and a firm hand gripped his upper arm and helped him to his feet. She poked his arm and said, "Open your hand" Harbal felt pills drop into his palm. "Antihistamines, it'll help with the itch and swelling. And the next time I put you someplace, be mindful and stay there." Harbal downed the pills. Again, she grabbed a fistful of his shirt to start walking and staggered him back to the car. She opened the trunk. When he heard the trunk lid, he halted. "What?" he said, Myrtle pointed to the trunk. Harbal could barely see her face but, followed her arm down to the trunk. But Harbal, still in a state of swollen stupidity, mumbled, "Nomph, mime driving," and grabbed Myrtle's arm, and with his eyes swollen shut, he did not see the second lightning-fast roundhouse. Harbal woke in the trunk, bound hand and foot once again. At least she hadn't taped his mouth shut this time. But of course, there was no need to tape anything on his face after a night of being blanketed by hungry insects. His face resembled a badly worn soccer ball and his nostrils stuttered with each tiny intake of air. Harbal was fuming.

Myrtle drove on and stopped several times to open the trunk and pour water over Harbal. He sputtered and swore at her so, when he de-swelled enough that she could understand him, she taped his mouth shut again. "Nobody likes a foulmouthed asshole," she said as she slammed the trunk lid, stalked back to the driver's seat, climbed in and hit the gas raining the heavy toolbox down on him again. She was in a real snit. Harbal never had much experience with women, and now that he was getting lessons, he wondered how the entire human race had survived.

Myrtle drove for most of the following day, with occasional stops for snacks. to water the moron in the truck and then by diner time turned the car down another dirt road into the deep woods. This road was not quite as smooth as the last dirt road, and it jostled and rearranged more tools on Harbal's head for nearly an hour before coming to a halt. Harbal heard the engine stop and the driver's door open, crunching dirt, and then the trunk lid lifted to reveal a beautiful sunset somewhere deep in the mountains. Myrtle was standing over him, cigarette hanging from her mouth. She waited until she saw his eyes focus.

"Now son, I will remove your bonds again to see if you've learned anything. If you try to run it will cost you, and I gotta tell you this since you seem to have the IQ of a baby-rattle. NEVER mess with an older woman. Women don't get to be older by being weak or stupid. An older woman has seen some things beyond your understanding and can turn a man inside out and iron him like a shirt if she's got a mind to. So, all the muscles you have in your arms are worthless because that sort of strength won't help you. You need to migrate those muscles into your head. So, when I cut your bonds, you will climb out of this trunk, gather some firewood and stay where I can see you. Do we have an agreement?" Harbal stared at her through still swollen eyes. But as she watched him, she could see the emotions swirling inside them. This was a good sign because yesterday, his eyes were dead. "Good," she said to herself and swiftly sliced through his bonds.

Dinner was hot dogs roasted over an open fire. Harbal just stared at the fire holding the stick. He refused to look at her and said nothing while the fire flared up with the juices that sizzled and dripped. Still totally lost and confused in his view of this situation, he figured she was simply driving him far enough away from his last known location so his body, if found, would not lead back to her. Myrtle sat quietly with her paper cup and studied the thoughts swirling across Harbals face as the fire slowly died down. He could not yet be trusted she knew, so he went back into the trunk for the night. He was hesitant to obey, but that little knife of hers glittered in the firelight as she used it to clean her nails. So, when she said "trunk" Harbal complied.

8) Learning The Fun De'mentals.

Myrtle reached down to pour a drop of Gin into her morning coffee sitting beside the fire. Harbal drank stream water, stream water suited him just fine, for all his mistakes, taking up the drink was not one of them. After about an hour of his silence, Myrtle stood up and stretched.

"You been cramped up in that trunk a long time. You need some exercise," she said as she walked toward the car.

Harbal stopped chewing his cold pop tart and paused, only God knew what this crazy old woman meant by 'exercise.' He thought to himself. Harbal dared not move away from where he sat until he knew he'd get the upper hand; he had come to understand that there was a great deal more to Myrtle than her colorful Muumuu would reveal. She returned from the car with a softball.

"Let's play 'catch'" she said. Harbal looked dumbfounded. The only thing he had ever played 'catch' with was his mother heading for him midair like a locomotive. He had never done this ball-tossing garbage. Myrtle tossed the ball up and down playfully in her hand.

"Well, get up, boy, let's get some exercise." So, he cautiously stepped out into the clearing. Myrtle took her stance on the other side and gently tossed the ball to Harbal, who let it hit his chest and fall to the ground without moving.

"Are you going to kill me?" he asked with the ball at his feet.

Myrtle replied, "..." That depends on if you pick up that ball and toss it back like a good boy."

"What if I decide not to be a good boy?" Harbal replied. Myrtle gave out a heavy sigh.

"Well, that pretty much sums it up don't you think, what you DECIDE, because so far you ain't been making good decisions. Pick up the ball, bonehead," she said with an evil smirk.

So Harbal picked up the ball. He tossed it back at her like a six-yr old. It landed several feet from her, and she had to walk over and pick it up. She stood up, looking tired, and tossed the ball back to Harbal. Again, he just let it hit his chest and fall to the ground with another soft thud.

"Where are you taking me?" he asked.

Myrtle folded her arms and stared at him. Neither one of them moved. Harbal bent down and picked up the ball.

"Where are you taking me?" he repeated, tossing the ball up and down with the same menace that Myrtle had used.

"I'm not at liberty to say at this time," Myrtle replied.

Harbal tossed the ball to her this time. She caught it clumsily in both hands.

"There now, that's much better. She said, tossing the ball back to him; this time, he caught it and tossed it back.

"Excellent," Myrtle replied, and she returned the ball to Harbal in a casual toss. Ok, you're catching on now; toss it back again," she smiled.

Harbal looked down at the ball. It was a blunt object made of solid material. He was a strong man, he had an exceptional aim, and He was in dire straights being carted across the country in the trunk of a car by a mob maw who was simply seeking a safe place to hide his body when she tired of this game she was playing. Harbal held the weapon in his hand knowing this was his last chance at freedom. If he killed her at this point, who would blame him, and who would find her..., who in hell would even look? He would take the car and drive to a new life. Harbal settled a lethal focus on Myrtle, then took aim and hurled the ball at her face hard enough to pass through her skull and embed itself in the tree trunk somewhere in the woods behind her. A thrill of delight blossomed in his mind as he saw his little white ball of freedom rapidly closing the distance to Myrtle's face. In a split second, he would be driving her car off into the sunset, leaving no trace of her existence behind. A free man, out of the reach of...

She caught the nearly invisible ball directly in front of her face with one bare hand. No flinching, no yelping, and she was smiling. Harbal stumbled backward. His eyes were wide. He was stunned to a blank incredulous stare; he had tried to take her out, and she was just holding that little projectile of death and smiling like it was a bouquet' of roses. And then, the look on her face turned to pure evil.

"Son, do you really want to keep sleeping in that trunk, wouldn't you rather be sitting upright and watching the beautiful scenery pass by?" Harbal stammered in shock and then just reacted.

"Drop Dead Hag!" Harbal shouted at her in angry frustration. Myrtle shook her head sadly. Once again, Harbal wasn't thinking things through. She raised her eyes, looking at him.

"Son, first of all, you just disrespected an older woman what I warned you never to do, Secondly, you did it after you threw away the only usefully weapon you had, and thirdly.... you showed me how YOU throw like a girl, but you ain't seen how I throw. You have expressed your entire philosophy of life in less than one second and confirmed it in three words, which is why you spend so much time in reverse." ... And before the last word evaporated in the crisp mountain air, a large white mass was directly in front of Harbal's face. Harbal woke up in the trunk. His nose was bleeding, and his shirt was bloody, but she had not duct-taped him up this time. He was safe to move freely about the inside of the trunk as the car causally wound its way around and through the mountains of West Virginia. Harbal reached up and felt the lump that grew from the bridge of his nose to his forehead; It was the exact same size as a softball. His head hurt, and every car bounce sent lightning bolts through his vision. He was delighted that he had never played this 'catch' game with his father.

9) Making Friends With Wildlife.

They did not stop for dinner that evening. Myrtle kept her eyes on the road, tossed pistachios into her mouth, and chewed. Harbal was not getting dinner this time either. She figured that he probably couldn't chew after she hit him with the softball anyway. In the meantime, Harbal, swollen black and blue, dazed, confused and hungry, lying in a dark car trunk amidst the tools and jack stands, started questioning his decision-making paradigm. It may be possible that Myrtle had a point, that going in the wrong direction was not providing him with the right stuff. Harbal wondered where he would be now if he had just played ball with her as she had asked. He wondered what would have happened if he had just worked the job in the car parts store and not stolen the parts; last but not least, Harbal wondered what would have happened if he had smothered her before he tried to steal her shoeboxes. He knew the answer to that question now. He had underestimated her. If he had actually tried to harm her, he was pretty sure he would be fertilizing her petunias.

Harbal closed his eyes against the pain in his head and went to sleep. He dreamt of the little girl this time for some reason. She was sitting in the trunk with him, holding his hand, always so quiet, looking into the horizon, looking into the future he might have had. He could feel her touch, and his entire body relaxed into it. With this simple dream filling his troubled mind, and in spite of the jack-stands and toolbox's, he fell into a deep sleep for the first time in many empty years. When he woke, the trunk lid was open and there was a blanket lying on the ground beside a campfire. Myrtle was stirring a small pot of stew made from things she had found in the surrounding forest, like mushrooms, edible plant bud stems, and tubers. She added a pinch of salt, tipped the wooden spoon to her mouth, and smiled at the result. Harbal climbed out of the trunk and staggered to the blanket where he took a seat.

"Oh, there you are boy," Myrtle exclaimed. "Good to have you back."

Harbal's eyes hurt as he squinted at the pot in the coals, there was still a large black mass between his two black eyes. He resembled a raccoon.

"Glad you made it for dinner this evening." Myrtle added.

She shoveled some of the concoction into a paper bowl, sat it on the ground before Harbal, and stuck a spoon into his hand. He wasted no time getting to the dinner. Myrtle may have been a dangerous enigma, but she could cook. Harbal wolfed down the stew, wiped his mouth on his arm and tossed the paper bowl aside. Myrtle looked at him over the top of her spoon.

"Son, be mindful of what you leave for others, pick up that bowl and place it in the trash, please."

Harbal's first reflex to her authority had gotten him the blackened goose egg between his eyes, and the same knee jerk reaction had landed him in jail too many times. He never seemed to be able to make the right choice. But in the last couple of days, he had had time to examine his choices. So, he stood up, retrieved the bowl, and placed it into a large black plastic trash bag Myrtle had placed beside their camp. She smiled.

"Now, son," she said, "there ain't no point in running from here. These woods are filled with wildlife that ain't quite as nice as those mosquitos. So, stay close to the fire and don't leave my sight."

Harbal rolled his eyes. Here comes another bad decision. He smiled to himself, stood up from the fire, and started walking into the woods. He did not hear Myrtle get up or shout; she just sat there smiling as he disappeared into the gloom of the wooded canopy. He also smiled for the first time since this nightmare began, freedom was his. The old lady could not outrun him, and she was already too far behind. Harbal could smell freedom tinged with the scent of pine needles, fresh air and the handful of hotdogs in his pocket he had purloined for his exit. He began to trot through the woods every foot fall taking him further from death via Myrtle and her odd sense of humor. The wind in his face was exhilarating as the trees blurred past him.

Myrtle remained by the fire smiling to herself. She figured that either he was going to take a leak, or he was going to run. Either way, he would be back in camp in a few minutes. Myrtle sipped some gin in her little paper cup and waited. Two minutes passed, then five, and then somewhere in the distance she heard the scream. Poor dumb boy, she thought to herself. She stood up, stretched, and walked into the woods in the same direction as the screaming. She started to chuckle. In about five minutes, she came to a clearing, and there he was, halfway up a young tree with a fairly large brown bear at the base shaking it.

Myrtle folded her arms and just watched. Every time the bear shook the sapling, it would come back and hit the knot already on Harbal's head. He clung to the trunk desperately as his head kept making contact with the trunk tock tock tock. Little squeals of misery escaped him each time. TOCK.

"OOooh, that's gotta hurt," Myrtle said each time he connected with the trunk. The tock, swish, tock swish, swish tock sound gave her giggles, as did his shouts of pain. When it looked like the bear was winning, she shouted to Harbal...

“Son, got food on you somewheres?”

Harbal grimaced and yelled “Yes”

“Then you gotta let go of that sapling and throw that stuff away from you. Mr Bear ain’t gonna stop rattling you until that food falls out.”

Harbal struggled to free one arm from the small trunk, then fished the hotdogs out of his shirt and hurled them away. Myrtle grabbed the sides of her Muumuu and began flapping them and making weird noises. The bear's head spun around in alarm, and when he saw that vision, he backed away from the tree and loped out across the clearing toward the hotdogs, grabbing them up as he ran into the shade of the forrest on the other side. Harbal fell out of the tree. He sank to the ground and sat there dazed and shaking. He was holding his head in both hands. The only bears he had ever known wore ballet skirts, rode bicycles, drank beer, and ate lunch at the same table as the other crew members.

"So, what's it gonna be tonight boy, trunk or tent?" Myrtle asked as he submissively followed her back to camp. Harbal looked at her incredulously and then stared in the direction the bear had cantered. He chose the trunk.

"Ah, yes...good decision, very practical," Myrtle said, turning back toward camp. Harbal followed her in silence, staggering slightly and holding his head. When they reached the camp, he went and stood by the trunk. Myrtle tossed in the blank he had been sitting on earlier and he climbed back into the trunk unaided. Harbal asked her quietly,

"Where are you taking me?"

"Why...home son," she replied., "I'm sending you home."

The trunk lid closed on her words, and Harbal was again in darkness. He lay there for hours, rolling that word over in his mind. He had no home; he has never had a home. Circuses move constantly. There was never a 'home, and even if there was a 'home' Myrtle could not know where his home was, and as a matter of fact, neither did he. So where was this 'home' she spoke of? In a slow creeping realization, it occurred to him that there were several ways to 'go home,' and pine boxes were one of them. The rest he was not so clear on, since no place by that definition had ever existed truly existed for him. He fell asleep thinking about the girl. He hoped he would dream of her tonight, but instead, he dreamt of gigantic bears, which was prophetic considering that sometime in the wee hours of the morning, while the air was thin and the darkness clung to the sleeping world in silence, a large set of claws slammed into the trunk lid bouncing the car, rending the lid into wide strips, and sinking three inches through the metal in front of Harbal's terrified eyes. The metal ripped open wide enough for him to see through clearly at the face of the bear he had encountered earlier that evening. He screamed like a little girl. He heard Myrtle yelling "yalp yalp, woooeeeeeee yalp yalp scat scat scat...." There was a loud snort, a sort of scream, and then rustling outside the trunk, and in another couple of minutes, it opened. Myrtle looked down at him.

"Got food in there with you?" she asked.

Harbal opened the toolbox lid to reveal several granola bars he had pinched from Myrtle's stash in the back seat along with the hotdogs. One bar was half eaten; the wrapper folded over.

"That'll do it alright," she said., "Time to go," and she unlocked the truck moving off to begin breaking camp.

Harbal climbed out of the trunk to help her. He wanted away from there at once. He kept swiveling his head for signs of the bear. They folded up her tent and lowered the cooler down from the tree. She packed everything back into the back seat and opened the passenger door signaling for him to sit in the front. Harbal stared at the passenger seat with longing, then his eyes drifted up to Myrtle, and he climbed back into the trunk. He had things to think about. Myrtle chuckled as she closed the lid and climbed in behind the wheel.

10) It's The Little Things That Matter Most

They had been on the road for hours when the car once again entered rough terrain bouncing and jostling over a dirt road. Harbal slept right through the ride. When the trunk lid opened, he was dreaming of the girl again, when Myrtle shook him awake and handed him a cold Pepsi. He rubbed his eyes and took the can from her hands. "What do you say, boy?"

Harbal looked at her blankly and said, "where's the sandwich? She clocked him on the head. "Ouch.".

"What do you say, boy?" she repeated. ... " What do you say when someone shows you kindness?" Harbal was really lost now.

"Ah, actually, I don't know that I've ever seen it," he replied.

Myrtle reached in and took the can of Pepsi away.

"Hey..." he started.

"What do you say when someone is kind to you?" she asked again holding the delicious ice-cold drink away from his reach.

Harbal thought for a minute and reluctantly said, ..." "Thank you?"

She handed him back the Pepsi and said, “Saying thank you," is another step toward being less of an asshole, recognizing that not every person in the world is a mark and that most people perform kind acts for appreciation, even if it shouldn't be that way. From now on, you will consider everything I do to you as an act of kindness and thank me for it. After all, I could have killed you in New Jersey and hung your mutilated corpse on a light pole in the middle of Mount Holly, and no one would have blinked." Harbal was at full attention after that last comment. What she was saying was true, and he knew it. He was convinced she could kill him while casually sipping her gin and eating her pistachios. She was one very scary and unpredictable old dame, and he couldn't figure out why he could not get the best of her. He was undoubtedly bigger, which meant he had to be stronger, but no matter what he did, he could not escape her short of wringing her neck. Maybe that's what was wrong, he wasn't trying hard enough, or maybe She was from Mars, he thought. Almost as if she had read his thoughts, she snagged the rope out of the trunk, walked to the nearest pine tree, bit the rope in her mouth, wrapping her arms tightly around the narrow trunk, then her legs and shinnied up the tree to tie off a line to hang lanterns and coolers. This was a vastly mind-expanding sight for Harbal. She was in her Muumuu fifteen feet above the ground, legs wrapped around the tree and tying off the lines like a professional rigger. Harbal was flabbergasted again. He had been taught to do that himself for setting up lantern lines for the big top. Who in hell was this woman, and how did he get here? When her feet hit the ground, Harbal was standing in front of her.

"Who are you?" he demanded.

Myrtle looked up at him and smiled.

"I am Ms Myrtle," she replied as she stepped around him.

He stepped back in front of her.

"I asked you a polite question, you owe me a polite answer," he said.

Myrtle stared into his chest.

"Fair enough," she said. She looked up at him and said,

"Excuse me, but I am not at liberty to reveal that to you at this time."

Harbal lost it. It was time to get serious and try harder. He grabbed her by the throat in an iron grip.

Harbal missed dinner that evening while he slept in the trunk, duct-taped into the fetal position. He sure was a stubborn boy. And when he woke, he had a sharp, debilitating pain in his loins. A slow realization and regret clawed its way up his spine as he remembered grabbing her by the throat. What had come over him? He remembered the searing pain that exploded from his neither region while she hardly moved and kept smiling at him over his big squeezing hands. Now there was not one square inch left on his body that did not ache. His face was still swollen from the softball, and now everything below his waist felt like the grounds of a sports stadium after a riot; his goalpost would not be standing up again any time soon.

The smooth ride he was getting in the trunk indicated that the car was on a freeway. Harbal felt the rhythm of the cement joints every few seconds. They hurt. He could also hear muffled singing from the front of the car and police sirens. Inexplicably, it occurred to him that this could amount to a rescue. He found himself torn between screaming for help, which meant returning to the big house for parole violations or staying quiet and rotting on the floor of a pine forest somewhere in the southwest. After the last few days on the road with Myrtle, Harbal opted for the big house; at least he could fight back there. In prison, the criminals were slow and stupid, all fists and fury, no brains. Having all that AND brains made Myrtle the most dangerous person he had ever met. He chose prison.

He felt the car slow and pull off to the shoulder and felt it gliding to a stop. Then the crunch of boots on cinders beside the car. The exchange between the cop and Myrtle, was not what he had expected.

"Well good morning Ms Myrtle" the Cop said as he stepped up to the driver's window.

"What in the world happened to the lid of your trunk?" he asked.

"Oh, I went camping last night and bumped into a bear." Myrtle replied. "He was looking to eat something." She added casually.

Harbal was lying stunned in the trunk over the exchange he was hearing. The officer then asked her what on earth she had in the trunk of her car that a bear wanted to eat, and Myrtle replied,

"One of my tenants who tried to rob me" She stated matter-of-factly.

Harbal felt a thrill of panic wrapped in confusion shoot through his entire body. Then He saw the face of the officer lean over checking him out through the tears on the lid. The Cop just shook his head.

This can't be right thought Harbal. The guy is still a Cop, and all Cops want is to arrest people and Harbal was wanted for parole violations. So Harbal started kicking the lid to the trunk to get the Cops attention. It didn't work. He had feared from the start that the Mob was involved, and he now figured this Cop was one of them. The Cop stood there for several more minutes conversing with Myrtle and making several disturbing comments about ridding the planet of people stupid enough to take advantage of a good women like Myrtle.

"Good woman"? Harbal screamed through the duct-tape. He kicked the trunk lid again shouting muffled obscenities. The officer Said,

"Keep it down in there mister and watch your mouth."

Staring wide eyed through the rips in the lid, Harbal saw the Cop tip his hat, and say,

"It's a lovely evening for a drive, Ms Myrtle," and then he walked back to his patrol car. Harbal heard him pull off and leave the scene.

Harbal was confused and flabbergasted again. He had always been able to count on the constabulary to haul him into a nice clean jail with three hots and a cot. For him, jail time was like daycare compared to what Myrtle had in store. But now, Harbal knew that all hope was lost, and his fate was inexorably tied to this crazy landlady and her frightful cross-country adventure that would almost certainly end in his demise. He was now in new mental and emotional territory and at the mercy of the menace behind the wheel. He was helpless. Nothing he knew could work to free him from her clutches. Prison had been so much easier. Harbal began to sink into a deeper state of confusion and despair. He worked his duct-taped wrists under the jack stand and retrieved the granola bar. As he struggled to unwrap it, he said, "Thank you" to no one in particular, then carefully put the empty wrapper back under the jack-stand.

Harbal was under the lid for a long time this time. The old woman must be pissed. He didn't make a sound for fear of further reprisals; he probably would not survive any more injuries. Around the fifth hour, the car pulled over, and Myrtle opened the trunk lid.

Harbal flinched away from her. He saw the stiletto flip upside down in the air and braced himself for the end. She sliced through his bindings like a surgeon again, then handed him a cold Pepsi and a ham sandwich. She leaned on the fender, eating her sandwich while he unwrapped his. He stopped unwrapping the sandwich as he remembered his last lesson and said,

"Thank you for the sandwich and Pepsi, I guess you're pretty mad at me."

Myrtle's eyes were on him. They were hard. They could have been the hardest eyes he had ever stared into. He winced involuntarily. It's not like he was softening toward her or anything; it was more that he was scared senseless of what she could and would do to him next. He kept thinking about the softball, her right hook, the look of terror on the face of the bear, the friendly conversation with the Cop, and was sweating at the reality of her capabilities. He had never felt so absolutely helpless at the hands of another person. He could always find someplace to hide or some way to escape. But not this time. This time he was trapped inside a dark car trunk with the most dangerous enemy he had ever met: HIMSELF.

Myrtle said nothing as she stared at him and chewed. When she had finished her food, folded up the wrapper and crushed the Pepsi can she said,

"Finish your food inside," We'll be on the road all night. I want to get through Kentucky by daybreak. The sooner I'm done with you, the better."

Harbal ducked down in the trunk just as the lid slammed shut. She was in a foul mood. He finished his food in the trunk, watching the sky flicker past above the claw holes made in the trunk lid by the bear. The sun began to set, and the sky was streaked with orange. Lying there comfortably now, he began to notice the colors in the sky for the first time since he was a kid. In the summertime, he lay on top of the lion cage with a Pepsi and watched the sky change color as the sun went down. He remembered the vast and beautiful stars on the open plains. It was the only peaceful time he could remember, and like now, he felt the same sort of peace roll over him for some strange reason. When the sky darkened, he fell asleep, curled back up in that fetal position, and dreamt of the girl. She climbed in through a boxcar window. She was as light on her feet as a fly and sat beside him. She reached for his hand, and he reached for hers. They sat this way together until he heard the BOOM!

The car shook and limped off to the side of the road. He kept his eyes tightly shut, trying to hold on to his dream, but his mind was awake, and the girl slipped away with the evaporating fog of sleep. The car had blown a tire. When it stopped moving, he heard the driver's door open, the crunch of gravel, and Myrtle cursing up a blue streak. The trunk lid flew open, and she reached in around his back and yanked out the jack stands. There was a temporary spare tire under the lid where Harbal lay.

"Up," she said. He was out of the trunk like lightning. She pulled up the trap door and revealed the spare tire, several bottles of gin, more rope, and some bottled water. Harbal reached in and pulled out the tire. He rolled it to the side of the car where Myrtle was already placing the jack to lift the car high enough to get the tire off. The new tire was temporary and not fit to drive further than, say, Texas. So, they would have to stop in civilization somewhere soon. Harbal smiled to himself, apparently all was not lost after all. Civilization=escape. Myrtle watched as Harbal fitted the lug nuts back into place and tightened them down. He wiped his hands on Myrtles Muumuu, and she slapped him away. Crickets sang in the southern woods as he snapped the hubcap back into place, and they were good to go for a few more miles. Harbal looked down and realized the tire iron was next to his foot. A small light came on in his eyes. He slowly reached forward, not raising suspicion, and pulled the tire iron back into his hand. When he looked up at Myrtle, the familiar stiletto touched the end of his nose. "Boy, you sure are hard to learn. How do you want to arrive at your final destination, facing your final fate like a man, or bleeding out in the trunk, 'cause it ain't no skin off my nose either way." Harbal gently placed the tire iron back where it was and, without saying one word, climbed back into the trunk. The tools landed on top of him.

The lid slammed shut, and in a few minutes, the car began to move once again. At least he wasn't duct taped. He had to get control of his mindless knee-jerk impulses before she lost patience and really killed him.

11) Motel 6 ¾

They drove until sunset. Myrtle stopped when they entered a small town where tires could be repaired, and groceries could be restocked. Harbal woke when he felt the car bump the curb in a parking lot. He had not dreamt of the girl again. That made him feel isolated and sad. Harbal could see snatches of the motel sign through the holes ripped in the car trunk as the vehicle stopped. The driver's door opened, and he heard her footsteps fading in the distance. Myrtle had driven the car into a motel parking lot and entered the office to get a room. She chose a double room on the third floor and at the end of the walk. When she returned, she opened the trunk and simply said, "Out." He did so at once. And she took him up the steps and into the room on the end. It was a shabby place with faded wallpaper and worn furniture. There was one double bed against the wall, and an old, faded wing chair by a double glass door which led to a small balcony. An air conditioner held in place with a bungie cord rattled in one side window. Above the bed was a painting of a bucolic countryside filled with sheep who were every bit as threadbare and lethargic as the room.

"Pick a spot," Myrtle commanded. Harbal chose the wing chair closest to the sliding glass doors, where he had a lovely view of the twinkly lights that festooned the sewage plant next door. Then Myrtle tossed a bag on the bed and pulled out the rope. "The rope."

The rope Harbal had feared from the start, after all, people frequently commit suicide in motel rooms just like this one.

"I'll behave," Harbal said.

"Sure, you will," was the answer.

"What are you going to do?" he asked.

Myrtle flicked open her lighter and lit a cigarette.,

"You ask a lot of questions for a guy who ain't gonna get any answers. You should be thankful I'm not leaving you in the trunk in this heat."

"I've come to like the trunk," Harbal answered. Myrtle stood there holding the rope in one hand and the glowing lighter in the other and stared at him with disdain.

"Listen son, I don't want to knock you out anymore, you've already had too many blows to your head and I'm afraid you'll be too brain damaged to be useful for anything but a doorstop before I can get this over with. So let me tie you up, so you can't go making any bad decisions while I'm gone. We both know you can't control your impulsive behavior and never use your head for anything besides growing hair. I need to get the tire fixed and shop for more groceries in town and I might need the trunk."

"So where are you taking me?" he asked.

"Oh, for crying out loud boy."

She picked up the table lamp and shook it at him. Harbal sat stock still and nodded, then held out his hands for the rope.

"That's better,"

she mumbled, tying his hands with a 'mooring hitch; she ran the rope under the seat of chair, up the back and down under the chair again to secure him back in the seat. She gave in enough slack to use his arms but not enough to reach anything important. Then she ran the rope over the arms of the chair and around Harbal's thighs so the rope would not cut off the circulation and make his feet fall off. This way he could also stretch his legs. As she worked Harbal sat still trying to look innocent. Myrtle watched his face, and smiled to herself, so she wrapped the rope one more time around Harbal and the chair, and as she bent down to tie it behind the back, she realized that the chair was just sitting there on the floor and not anchored. Now Harbal was trying to look fearful and timid. Myrtle had to stifle a laugh. She straightened up holding the rest of the coil of rope and stared at the back of Harbals innocent head.

"Au Huh" she murmured,

Then she crossed to the bed and tied the rope around the bed frame that was bolted to the floor. Standing up she dusted off her hands and stared at Harbal again. He could move his arms and hands but could not undo the knots. He could flex his legs but go nowhere and no matter what hijinks he was plotting in his tiny little brain, He would be safe and comfortable until she got back.

Meanwhile, Harbal sitting perfectly still watched Myrtle tie knots. He watched her with dismay, because he knew those knots; Harbal had tied those knots as a kid, and he also understood that he was going nowhere under the control of those same knots. His best course of action would be to start screaming the minute she left. Myrtle was watching these thoughts scroll across his face like a marque, so she rolled down one of her socks and took it off, holding it up for him to see. Then she held up the duct tape, "Do I stuff a dirty sock in your mouth or just tape it shut?"

"I'll take the tape and keep my mouth shut."

“Good boy” She muttered and then added, “by the way; you’re wanted in this state too” Harbal straightened up in the chair. He was so intent on planning his escape he had forgotten.

"Smart boy."

She slapped a strip of duct tape over his mouth, turned on the TV, adjusted the air conditioner, set two open bottles of water on the small table beside Harbal’s chair and left. Harbal sat there for several minutes looking resigned. When he was sure she was gone, he began to study the double glass doors. They were latched. He was in a third-floor corner room with two doors, one was the entrance, and the other was a small cement balcony surrounded by a freshly painted black wrought Iron railing. His plan was to get that door open, and get himself out onto the porch, kick the glass door out and use the broken glass to cut himself loose. It was already after 6 PM so he would escape under the cover of darkness. He was wanted in this state also and the jails here were not as civilized as the ones further north, and why should he suffer either if he could break free of both. So, he did not want to draw too much attention to his escape. He turned up the sound on the TV. Then he started to push his chair around to see what sort of range he had. Harbal pushed the chair closer to the center of the double door. Then he turned the chair by hopping until he was facing the door straight on. The door was latched with a standard sliding glass door latch. Harbal studied this latch closely because without being able to reach it with his hands, he would have to use his feet. He was wearing work boots. The only choice he had was to try and kick the handle out of the way so he could push the latch with his boot. He slowly and carefully pushed his chair back far enough to be able to curl his leg up to kick the door handle.

All actions have an equal and opposite reaction. The chair flew over backwards and hit the floor, banging his head on the thinly carpeted cement. Harbal scrunched his eyes shut as the painful lump began to rise from his skull. A bugs bunny cartoon was on TV and Elmer Fudd was squweemin at dat waskelly wabbit. When all the tiny birds and stars stopped swirling around his head, Harbal rocked the chair from side to side trying to get up enough momentum to turn himself over onto his hands and knees. He actually succeeded after about ten tries. And now, he was on his hands and knees with a chair tied to his back. From this position he was able to push up with his fists, rise up on his knees and push the chair back upright with him in it. He laughed in triumph. Harbal once again maneuvered the chair directly in front of the door and took a look at the handle. His kick had broken the handle, and it hung out from the door and to one side giving him a shot at the latch. This he considered to be another small triumph; and with the latch exposed he tried every way he could to reach it. It occurred to him that if he tipped the chair back over again, he could use his foot to kick the latch and slide the door open. So, he moved the chair as close to the door as possible and pushed the chair up with his feet. The chair would not go over. Harbal pushed the chair back a couple more inches and then tipped it back and braced for the fall. The back of his head tapped the cement floor with and ouch. He lifted his right foot and pushed at the latch until it opened! Then he pushed door out of the way. He lay there enjoying that isolated moment of success. He could feel the warm night air wafting through the open door, and it smelled like freedom.

Harbal began to rock the chair sideways until he could get it turned over, but the chair changed its angle each time. Rolling sideways back and forth around the room, Harbal found himself between the closet and the dresser. The chair was proving to be very difficult to steer; and Harbal becoming frustrated. He tried to rock the chair hard to the right and away from the dresser, but it turned sideways again and hit the dresser hard enough to dislodge the small free standing flat screen TV, which immediately toppled off the dresser toward his face but was caught by the cord, where it jerked to a halt six inches from Harbals head. He lay stock still staring at the the fat screen inches from his cranium, and then laughed. HA! He muttered through the duct tape. "Saved by the... The cord tore out of the back of the TV and several exciting things happened at once.

First the flat screen rapidly closed the distance to Harbal's face, which flattened his nose and started a swelling around his eye, cut his eyebrow and then slide off his person to the floor. then the open elect cord, which was now swinging wildly with its first taste of freedom, came into contact with Harbal's pants. He felt an alarming jolt like he had been kicked in the leg, and then he noticed that his pants were on fire. He began rolling and bucking frantically in the chair; the more he tried to roll the chair out of the way of the cord, the more he hit the cord. The electric wire jumped and flew at him from every direction like a charged fire hose. The more it jolted him the more he screamed and jumped and every time he jumped, he'd hit the wire sending it flying again and something else on his person would light up and often catch on fire. Harbal had bitten through the duct tape and was still screaming when the chair finally rolled onto its side and the cord caught a small patch of fabric on the back of the chair.

Once the chair was on its side, Harbal, panting and gibbering like a maniacal chipmunk, began frantically throwing himself against the side of the chair until it turned over face down again. He lay for another minute as his muscles continued to jerk and jump and he smelled smoke, as the electric cord continued to swing around above him, he started frantically scooting the chair toward the double glass doors with his fists and knees. He reached the open door and grimaced at the pain in his knees on the door track, dragged himself, swollen eyes, cuts, burned holes and his giant smoldering chair over the finish line and out onto the small side porch. He took a deep breath and let his freedom wash over him like a caress. Why does Freedom always come with a cost. But now that he was halfway out of the room, all that was left for him to do was get a shard of broken glass to use to cut through his ropes. Piece of cake. He had come this far; he would make the distance. He put his now raw bleeding knuckles on the cement and pushed with both hands and then legs to right himself and the chair. He grimaced at the door track under his shins, but it was a small price to pay to get out of this situation. When Harbal righted the chair, the back legs came down on the inside of the room and he could not turn the chair around to kick out the glass. He could not scoot the chair forward past the raised track. He could not turn the chair.

For what seemed like forever, Harbal just sat listening to the crickets singing in the surrounding darkness before he started quietly crying. His tears mixed with blood ran down his face, fell and doused out some of the small fires that were still burning on his chest. Little thin curls of white smoke rose lazily from Harbals body.

He took a deep breath, closed his eyes, and just pushed the chair over backwards and toppled back into the cement floor of the room. The chair landed sideways facing the dresser. The electric cord still hung there exhausted from their battle but still ready to go another round if threatened. Harbal with small tears of frustration rolling down the sides of his face, once again rocked the chair sideways to get back on his knees and the chair continued to change direction each time. He found himself in every location except the double door. He rolled past the door, the bed, the walls and the dresser where he squealed and pushed frantically to stay away from the exposed wire and leaving little bloody prints everywhere his knuckles, face and knees met the carpet.

It took a while, but Lady luck must have taken pity, for on the twentieth time he got the chair over on his back and was again on his knees. Once he was in position, the long hard journey across the room began again, and this time he would keep his cool and not stand the chair up until both legs were on the same side of the track. He huffed and puffed and dragged himself inch by inch back across the room, over the blasted tracks and out onto the cement porch. Once outside, he crawled the chair slowly around to face the glass door and pushed himself back into the upright position. With one foot he reached out and slid the door shut so that he would only be kicking one pane. Harbal centered himself, pulled up one leg and kicked the door. It just rattled in the frame. He kicked it again and nothing. So Harbal backed the chair up against the iron railing and wedged it solid. This would give him a foundation so he could use both feet on the glass. Harbal kick the glass, and it rattled a lot harder. He kicked it with both feet, and door popped out of the frame, but the glass didn't break. It was that nice strong and freshly painted iron railing that broke instead. Harbal felt the chair suddenly lurch backwards and heard the iron railing crash to the cement deck on the second story below, it happened quickly but felt like slow motion to Harbal who was now air born out over the deck. He watched the cement slab that was his foundation grew small above as a sensation of weightlessness flooded him. He saw the broken rusty railing on his way past the second floor and that was when he fainted. The rope that Myrtle had had the good sense to tie to the bolted bed frame did its job and jolted the chair and its swooned occupant to a shocking halt six inches about the hood of a car, which had just pulled into the parking space. The chair swung wildly with its occupant dangling from the seat. The rush of air on the way down had refreshed the little fires on the fabric of the chair, as it swung back and forth above the hood of Myrtles car.

Myrtle had just arrived back at the motel and pulled into the space just below their room when the chair appeared from the sky and jerked to a sudden halt at the end of the rope in front of her. She sat in the car eating a SlimJim and staring at the sight just above her hood. She turned off the key and killed the engine. She sat there quietly chewing and watching the smoldering chair face down with an unconscious man, also smoldering, swing back, and forth, to and fro over the hood of her car. She finished the SlimJim, stuffed the empty wrapper in the ashtray, wiped her fingers on her dress and opened the car door. She walked up and looked at Harbal who was coming out of his swoon. His eyes were saucers when he saw where he was and as the chair dangled from the rope and twisted around, he saw Myrtle. She said nothing. She turned around, went back and opened the trunk to gather up the groceries and put them in the back seat. Then she climbed back behind the wheel and backed the car up making a lazy circle in the parking lot, then maneuvered the car directly under Harbal and the chair. Harbal whimpered as he swung helplessly back and forth staring at the ground and wishing he was under it already and this was over with. She was going to kill him soon he just knew it. He was so close to a clean get-away. Myrtle backed the car directly under Harbal and the chair. She got out walked casually back and opened the trunk lid making sure it tapped Harbal. He yelped. The chair spun. She stood there watching his predicament and pulled out and her stiletto, flipping it open with one smooth movement. She watched his eyes focus on the knife and she smiled. Then with deliberation making sure his eyes were on her, she turned and walked menacingly up the steps while staring at him and grinning maniacally. Harbal knew. He began screaming through the tiny bitten hole in the duct tape "NO! PLEASE NO!" But Myrtle kept climbing, slow and steady up the steps brandishing the knife. Tiny flickers of light from the streetlamp glittering on the blade, and then she disappeared into the room. Harbal tried to brace himself but how? He and the chair hit the trunk unceremoniously. Harbal face down on the floor of the trunk muttered 'thank you', saw stars, and blacked out. When he woke, the chair was gone. There was a bag of ice under his head, a blanket over him and the trunk lid shut. The car was back on the road. Myrtle was well rested after a good night's sleep in the double bed and had slipped the front desk a hundred dollars to affect the repairs to the room. Harbal spent the night safely in the trunk where he could make no more decisions. While he was out, Myrtle had dabbed him with burn cream, taped up some cuts and unceremoniously tore off his 5 O'clock shadow along with the duct tape she had applied over his mouth.

When Harbal woke in the trunk, his brains felt numb, his head hurt, both eyes hurt, he was covered in burns, and his lips were gone having been peeled away with the duct tape and 5 O'clock shadow, his hands and knuckles were rug- rash, his knees were raw and resembled the inside of a pair of small grapefruits, and he was swollen from head to foot. Every time he closed his eyes, he relived the sensation of falling backwards from a balcony three stories up while tied in a chair. He relived this riveting moment over and over and when the memory changed, he saw the TV set shooting toward his face and then the electric jolts all over him. In his sleep he kept rocking from side to side as he did try to right the chair. And in the end, he curled into the fetal position and began gibbering again. His easy escape had not gone as planned.

12) How To Develop A Healthy Relationship With Your Kidnapper Without Dying.

Later that afternoon Myrtle pulled off the road and opened the trunk to see if he still had a pulse. When the trunk lid flipped open, Harbal yelled, "THANK YOU," before Myrtle could utter a word. He was still alive after all and understood the significants of that since things had gotten out of his control early on. If being polite kept him alive after what he had already experienced, then he was gonna be the politest moron on the face of the earth. Everything she did to him should be considered kindness; he touched the salve on his raw forehead. He got it. He laughed manically out loud. It was an epiphany. He scratched a burned spot and winced as the carpet rash on his hands cracked. He had seen the light; he remembered his pants being on fire and chattered for a second like a terrified squirrel. He was a changed man and understood that he had gone stark raving mad. He and Myrtle would be best friends, two peas in a pod. Bahahahahhahaha. *Gasp. * Myrtle stood there watching this entire scene play out in the trunk.

"You're hysterical," she said flatly, and poured a bottle of water over him slamming the lid. He went back to sleep, woke with a jolt, back to sleep, woke with a jolt and finally slept. The sky flicked over his supine frame through the claw marks in the trunk. It was another lovely day for a drive. The next stop was a KOA campground in Arkansas. At the check-in desk, Myrtle requested the most remote campsite they had available; the site was located was at the bottom of a dry ravine, at the outer most reaches of the campground. The site was off grid with no plumbing or electricity. Myrtle didn't need facilities. She needed privacy. She didn't want any questions about the bear claw holes, or man in her trunk. Meanwhile, it was beginning to heat up in Arkansas, and Harbal had been in the trunk for a better part of a day recovering from his recent adventure with the wing chair. Myrtle had made pit stops, fed him lunch and gave him an occasional watering. He had continued to blither and giggle since that morning, and until he got a grip on himself again, Myrtle didn't want him on the loose in public. The bear claw holes gave him plenty of ventilation and sunlight. She parked the car at the bottom of the lowest point at the site where the air was coolest and prepared to set up camp. She opened the trunk lid and Harbal shouted, "Thank you," and grinned at her. She stood staring at his eyes. They were not empty anymore. Now they were deranged. She handed him a ham sandwich. He said, "Thank you," with the enthusiasm of a child, and then she handed him a Pepsi; he said, "Thank you" again with an eagerness that belied his temporary manic break down. So, Myrtle, being the kind playful soul she was and just for the hell of it, stepped around the side of the car and retrieved a dead squirrel she'd kicked aside while preparing the camp. She returned to the trunk and handed it to Harbal, who took it immediately and said, "Thank you."

"Ok, that's it, out of the trunk, you've had enough." She reached in to grip his arm, but he grabbed her instead, giggling maniacally, and pulled her into the trunk with him, yelling, "Thank You!" In the ensuing brawl, the trunk lid came down on its own, slamming shut with a terrifying 'click.' Both of them froze and stared at each other. Reason suddenly returned to Harbal's eyes. They were both locked in the car trunk on a hot Arkansas afternoon, in the middle of nowhere with a dead squirrel, and where no one could hear them screaming.

Myrtle shouted loudly directly into Harbal's ear. "YOU HAVE GONE STARK RAVING MAD YOU IMBECILE." "THANK YOU," he yelled back as if he thought she was deaf. Then Harbal did the unthinkable. He tried to hug Myrtle. (Expletive deleted) and she elbowed him in the eye and turned herself over on her back. She sized up the distance from her feet to the trunk took aim at the largest of the claw tears where the metal was weakest, and she began to kick the trunk lid. The weakened lid responded, and a small footprint appeared in the metal of the trunk. Myrtle started pushing out the holes the bear had torn. Harbal had covered his head with his arms to avoid her thrashing. She went at that truck lid with a rage so intense that Harbal saw visions of Armageddon.

He had been hit by her too many times and did not want to die just yet. In another couple of minutes, he would change his mind. Myrtle was plastered against him tirelessly kicking the trunk lid with legs like jackhammers. Every time she connected with the metal; she forced her back against him. Harbal started twisting away from her until he was face down and they were back-to-back. That was when he discovered where the dead squirrel had landed. With each kick, Myrtle forced Harbal into the dead squirrel, and with each face plant, Harbal shouted, "Thank you." Harbal was too big to curl his legs up and kick the trunk, so he helped Myrtle by playing dead.

By 2 PM, the trunk had heated up quite a bit claw marks and all with the Arkansas sun and the relentless kicking. The trunk lid had taken on a whole new appearance from the outside, as though many tiny nuclear devices had been detonated from within. Meanwhile, in the surrounding area, the noise caught the attention of the local fur-bearing residents. It brought in several curiosity seekers, like a bear, two foxes, and a dozen living squirrels, who were wondering why the two people locked themselves into a car trunk with their late Uncle Chuck. By 5 PM, the Buzzards had arrived in the treetops and were regurgitating snacks to share during the show. Meanwhile, 'Uncle Chuck's state of decomposition was becoming a problem for Harbal, who was rhythmically face-planted in his remains.

Harbal thought of the bolt cutters he had left under the bed at the boarding house and yelled, "Toolbox." Myrtle stopped kicking. The Buzzards, bears, foxes, and squirrels leaned in to watch. The car bounced about as Myrtle rearranged her position by elbowing Harbal's ear several hundred times and yelling at him for whining and being such a damn sissy. She reached the toolbox but could not lift the lid because there was no room. So, both she and Harbal tried to switch places, and each time his arm, hand, or face came in contact with a part of Myrtle, she somehow found the room to punch him. After a dozen of these blows, Harbal started punching back and saying, "Thank you," Within minutes, they were pummeling one another to the best of their ability in their cramped space. The car rocked about with the obscenities emitting from the claw holes in the trunk lid like fireworks, weaving a fabric of descriptive phrases so abhorrent they could have toppled trees like Mt Saint Hellens'. One mother squirrel reached over and clapped her hands over her youngster's ears. The spirit of Uncle Chuck, who was now smashed and spread evenly in layers over both combatants, reeked like the floor of a subway bathroom. The rocking and fighting tipped the toolbox enough that a chisel came out. They both stopped. Myrtle grabbed the chisel and face palmed Harbal's head out of the way. She turned her ire on the claw holes in the trunk and began to ratchet the tool back and forth and pushed the torn metal outward until she had created a frightfully jagged opening from one of the claw marks and began to kick the ragged sides of it open. She switched back and forth between the chisel and the kicking. Her hands and arms were scratched from the jagged metal, and her legs weren't much better.

Thunder clapped overhead.

Myrtle stopped kicking. Another roll of thunder rattled Myrtle's ribcage. "Holy mama," she said. It was just at the end of the dry season when the weather in this area could change rapidly. Myrtle gasped and kicked harder, driving her leg through the opening and out into the fresh air. She started with the chisel again to enlarge the hole another few inches. Then she rolled back and kicked the new opening a dozen times until the hole was wide enough for her to fit through. That was when it finally occurred to Harbal, who was now thoroughly smashed under her, that...

"Hey, you're not really old or fat."

Myrtle elbowed him in the throat and kept kicking. The thunder rumbled down the side of the mountain and large drops of rain began to hit the trunk. Flash flooding was common in the midwest; spillways, dry riverbeds, and culverts all came to life in a thunderstorm as the rain raced down mountain sides in search of low ground. Gravity was a real bitch. Meanwhile, back at the campground office, the people at the front desk had heard the thunder as well, and were concerned about the safety of the women who had asked for the remote site that would become a floodway in a matter of minutes. The thunderstorm hitting the mountains would send thousands of gallons of water down the spillway within the hour. Donald and Jonas who worked maintenance for the campground climbed into a Jeep and drove out to check on the old lady at the last campsite on the property. They took the shortcut down the wash to the location. The old lady in the Muumuu had been a strange one in the first place. Her car had bear claw marks across the trunk, and she was camping alone. As they drew closer to the site, a light wind that picked up delivered them a whiff of Uncle Chuck, and with the smell of something dead greeting them, all sorts of tabloid scenarios burst into their heads.

"What a great campfire story this might turn out to be for some long boring night." Joanas offered... "Camper tries to dispose of body at last camp site." But their laughter was filled with trepidation as they raced to the site. Rain was picking up now as large drops splattering the windshield. Their jeep pedal-to-the-metal, popped up over the ridge above the campsite just in time to see the head of the old woman in a shredded flowered Muumuu struggling to emerge from a jagged hole punched outward from her car trunk. It looked like the car trunk was giving birth to an alien. She was covered in bright pink flowers and bloody shreds of fabric and grunted like a hog to force herself through the jagged hole. The driver of the Jeep jammed his foot on the brake, nearly standing the vehicle on end. The Jeep came down hard on the ground, and both passengers nearly bounced from their seats. They watched in awe struck disbelief as a bloody woman in a shredded Muumuu, wild, gray-streaked hair emerged fully from the hole in the trunk lid, rolled off the car hood and fall to the ground, then she jumped up and stumbled to the driver's door where she climbed behind the wheel and started the engine. Then just as the car roared to life, a second human hand emerged from the same hole in the trunk. Myrtle hit the gas. The heads of the two men in the Jeep swiveled quickly to the right looking up the rise just in time to see a wall of water coming down the wash. It hit the car broadside just as Myrtle got it moving. She drove the car up over the low bank with the force of the water, onto the opposite side of the stream and just kept going through dense woods, bushes, and underbrush as saplings disappearing beneath the car. The men in the Jeep watched the baby blue 1998 Oldsmobile disappear into the gray rainy haze beyond, to the sound of snapping trees and a human hand still waving about from the rip in the trunk lid.

13) The Waffle House

Myrtle exploded directly onto Route 40 West from the damp woods, fishtailing slightly into the left lane. When she heard the sirens, she cursed and took the first exit ramp off the interstate, down the ramp, and into a Waffle House parking lot. She leaped out of the car in the pouring rain and released the trunk lid. Harbal said, "Thank you." She grabbed him by the shirt and pulled him out of the trunk. He came willingly. They both ran into the Waffle House, and Myrtle shoved Harbal into one of the retro red vinyl booths and sat across from him. She flipped up a menu to cover her face. Harbal, following her cue, did the same. The smell of burned grease and coffee only slightly masked the odor of Uncle Chuck, and they could hear the police sirens getting louder. All the heads in the restaurant turned and watched them when they entered. They were a sight to behold, both black and blue, soaking wet. Myrtle's Muumuu was nothing but tatters. They looked like they had spent the day in a cement mixer with a dead rodent.

A waitress, a large woman with walnut brown hair done up in a bun, and wearing a 'Waffle House T-shirt and black apron, came to the table with a frown. "You two connected to those sirens?" She asked. Myrtle cringed, looking up at her beseechingly, and said, "Yes, this is my son. We went out for a drive and got lost. My boy is hurt can you help us?" To Harbal's surprise, the waitress said, "Yeah, and maybe you can help us too, follow me into the back." Myrtle and Harbal were out of the booth and on her heels when the flashing lights and sirens arrived in the parking lot. The Waitress took them into the back where they had a slop sink and mops and told Harbal to hide in the bathroom until she came to get him. Myrtle was out of her tattered Muumuu before the bathroom door shut. She stepped into the slop sink, and waitress introduced herself as Bertha, and turned on the water to hosed her off from head to foot. Blood, mud rust, and torn fabric ran from her body and swirled around the drain at her feet. Bertha tossed her a towel. While Myrtle dried off, Bertha pulled Myrtle's gray-streaked hair back and tied it with one of her own ribbons. She handed Myrtle a Tee Shirt that said, "Waffle House" and pulled a pair of jeans off the hook with the aprons. Myrtle was pulling up a pair of blue jeans on her way back into the restaurant. Bertha handed her an order pad and pointed to a middle-aged couple in matching shirts already eating pancakes. They nodded yes.

"Give me your car keys, honey, and go take their order," she directed Myrtle.

Myrtle, no stranger to subterfuge and hi-jinks was overwhelmingly happy to participate in whatever wasn't her problem. She complied instantly and was nodding casually to the lovely couple and scribbling on her pad when the cops stopped circling her car and started towards the Waffle House. Myrtle watched them swagger toward the restaurant, and an ancient alarm rang in her gut. She kept her back to them when they entered. She knew bad cops when she saw them. Meanwhile, Bertha had hurriedly removed the half-eaten plates of food from two men who had sat in one corner of the counter. When these men saw the police approaching the restaurant, they hurried up from their seats, threw a $10 bill on the counter, and exited the side door just as the Cops entered the front. Bertha yelled at the police, pointing to the two men rapidly walking across the parking lot,

"Don't let them get away!!." The people in the restaurant joined in, pointing and nodding in agreement. The two men in the parking lot hearing a commotion inside broke into a run. The police are like puppies; if you run, they will chase you. The two police officers asked no questions about why they needed to stop the two men but burst out the side door after them in a run, caught them up, and tackled them to the ground. One of the people in the Waffle House, an elderly man in a gray tee shirt, had pulled out a cell phone the instant the cops had entered the restaurant and taped the encounter in the Waffle House parking lot. He recorded the two cops running at the men and tackling them. Then the cops began pummeling the men on the ground until neither moved. Their hands were pulled behind their backs, and cuffs were slipped into place. Still, the two police did not announce themselves, yell you're under arrest, they just gleefully beat and kicked them until they stopped crawling. One of the officers called for a tow to impound their vehicle while the other dragged the badly beaten men to the squad car.

Bertha turned to Myrtle." Honey, as soon as they leave, get your son and get all your items out of your car while Herb here: a white-haired man in kakis nodded, switches the plates and gets the guns and the traps and all the rest of their crap out of that truck. We will explain later." She handed Myrtle the keys she snatched from the counter when she took the men's plates. Myrtle didn't hesitate and took off for the car. Bertha returned to the back and got Harbal, who thanked her for opening the door. "Go help your ma," she said. Harbal ran like the wind to reach the car and help Myrtle switch her belongings. Myrtle was suspicious as to why he was so eager to cooperate. Normally he would be legging it down Route 40 for all he was worth. Harbal was wanted in Arkansas. He would rather not run into a cop who recognized him. He had come too far on this mysterious journey to have it end in a jail cell and no answers. He was now committed to this crazy relentless ride to purgatory no matter where it led.

Patrons who had been sitting peacefully in the restaurant eating their grits and waffles rose almost as one from their seats and filed out of the building. Every face was grinning from ear to ear. They were the locals who lived and worked, built families, worshiped, and died, all within a thirty-mile radius of the Waffle House. They were black, white, brown, yellow, red wore clothing they bought a

Walmart, and took care of one another in their community. They were just good people, and now they worked in tandem to solve a problem that Myrtle knew nothing about. Myrtle didn't care. Bertha told Myrtle it would take the cops twenty minutes to return with a tow truck and a squad of police. The local folks worked in unity with a cause, forming a bucket chain to get Myrtle's belongings out of her car and into the truck and vice versa. Myrtle watched her cooler, toolboxes, tent, blankets, bottles of gin, shovels, ropes, Piggly wiggly bags full of snacks, and cases of bottled water pass by her hand to hand. No one asked how her car came to be in its condition. They seemed to have a mission that was much bigger than Myrtle's cuts and Harbal's bruises. Myrtle and Harbal stood and watched as bloody bear pelts, guns, metal traps, nets, and baseball bats were switched along and tossed into their car. A man in a blue work shirt knelt by the car and switched the license plates, then everyone ran back inside the restaurant and took seats.

Bertha called Myrtle and Harbal over to sit at the front window with the rest of the regulars to watch the show when the cops arrived to impound the car. Bertha sat a plate of pancakes in front of both of them and a large serving of crispy bacon, telling them the chow was on the house. Myrtle and Harbal looked at each other and dug in. The tow truck arrived just under four minutes after the switch was complete. They all sat at the front tables and watched as the cops flooded into the parking lot and circled the car, guns drawn, with terrified expressions, staring at the mangled car in disbelief.

"Herb," Bertha called to her right, ... "poke Harvey." Turning to Myrtle, she said, "Harvey is deaf, but he reads lips."

Herb elbowed the man next to him who had ruddy brown skin after hard years on a tractor in the sun, he had a frayed baseball cap. He looked up at Myrtle and nodded his head. He began to interpret their arm waving, jabbering, and general overall behavior as they circled the car.

"They can't figure out what kinda animal those Bozo's had locked in the trunk that could rip out the metal and kill a bear. They're scared shitless," Herb said. Just as he finished, The Police chief's car pulled into the lot, and Bertha called:

"Harry... you're up." The man in the gray T-shirt who had recorded the altercation in the parking lot between the two officers and the two men, looked over at Bertha and nodded. Climbing from his seat he walked casually out to the group of police officers and handed his cell phone to the Chief. The Chief watched the video and raised his eyebrows, then lowered his eyebrows in a frown, then raised his eyebrows again as a tiny light seemed to come on in his eyes. The Chief patted Harry on the back and turned toward the Waffle House windows to nod to Bertha, who waved from the window. Myrtle crunched another piece of bacon and looked up at Bertha, who was smiling. Bertha looked down at Myrtle and said,

"Honey, those two boys are poachers who didn't care what they catch or shoot, your pets included. They are bad medicine, and we have been trying to catch them for two years. And those cops?" Bertha shook her head from side to side and added, "In the entire state of Arkansas, we have two bad cops and one bad Judge...all related. Harry here just taped the cops attacking two men without warrants, resistance, or questioning. So now, we got five rotten apples out of our city. Their cousin, the Judge, will be investigated and won't be saving their asses again this time. God must have sent you and your boy at just the right moment to get all of them in one fell swoop. We know you come from some sort of trouble, but we don't care how you come to rip open that trunk. That's your business, but maybe one day, when you find the time, you'll write me the story to explain. I'm sure it's a doozy and we can all share a good laugh." She placed her hand on Harbal's shoulder and said, "And we like your son; he is so polite. Every time you look at him, he says, '"Thank you.'"

Myrtle started choking on her mouthful of bacon, and Harbal reached around and pounded her on the back several times with enough force to break her ribs. "There, there 'MA,' don't be shy, you know you brung me up good." She glared at him, and he slid the silverware out of her reach.

14) Enjoying The Open

So, Myrtle and Harbal now scrubbed, fed, bandaged, and in clean clothes were back on the road, and entered the state of Oklahoma in a purloined pickup truck that they knew no one was in a hurry to check. Either from exhaustion or despair, they drove through the entire state in silence. Myrtle, eyes straight ahead, Harbal staring out the side window at the never-ending monotony of cactus, tumble weeds, saw grass and boulders that slid past the side of the truck almost as a blur. Both were lost in thought. Both struggling to understand what they had gotten themselves into. At 2 PM, Myrtle pulled over into a field, grabbed two sandwiches from her cooler in the back, and tossed one to Harbal. They sat on the tailgate of the green old Ford F150 and ate in silence. By nightfall, they had found another KOA campground and turned into the driveway. Myrtle requested a nicer site on the top of the ridge where they got a full view of the sun setting over the plains. She didn't have a man in her trunk at the moment, so felonies were no longer a consideration. The campsite was at the very top of the only ridge in the state. Myrtle parked the truck and climbed out, grabbing her gear as she walked past the truck bed. Harbal also grabbed a few of her things while he walked down the other side. Myrtle set up her tent and handed Harbal a pile of blankets. The sunset was lovely. They ate dinner in silence and turned in around

10 PM. Harbal had no trouble sleeping on the ground in the open. The stars were glistening in their heaven, and all was peaceful. In the silent splendor of the prairie his brain left panic mode and turned back on. The next day while they drove, Harbal broke the silence.

"Who's watching the boarding house while you chauffeur me off to the land of what-the-f**k?"

"Watch your mouth, you've been out of the trunk too long and it shows." Myrtle replied, her knuckles turning white on the steering wheel. Harbal stared out the passenger window at the endless flat landscape zipping past.

"Ms. Myrtle, may I ask who is watching the boarding house while we enjoy this endless vacation to southwest bumfuk?

She glanced over at him. "That's better, marginally better, but better. My sister is watching the house."

"Thank you" Harbal said with emphasis. "So, there is another one like you?" He asked.

"Oh, there are quite a few like me. I come from a very large family." Harbal blanched and stared straight ahead for a few minutes, trying to wrap his head around an entire herd of Myrtles all out there in the world, torturing people. Harbal's next question was the scary one. He took a deep breath and cleared his throat.

"Are you, by any chance, connected to the Mob?

Myrtle blinked, then she snorted, and then she said,

"Hell no, I ain't with the Mob. Those guys are wankers. If I were with the Mob, you would never have left my room after I caught you. Nah, no Mob" she laughed. Then she added," They came around once and made me an offer on my house. I told them no, and they threatened me. So, I beat their enforcer with a ball-peen hammer I was using to reupholster my couch, and they never came back. Myrtle laughed. Harbal blanched. Talk about going from the frying pan into the fire. Harbal was sorry he had asked, and before he opened his mouth to say another word Myrtle pulled the truck into a used car lot and stopped. Harbal gripped the door handle.

"You open that door, and I will drop you like a fat kid on a seesaw" Myrtle said under her breath. He let go of the handle. "We are changing cars. I don't like this truck. My things will get wet if it rains.

Harbal looked over at her. "We're in a desert. It doesn't rain here."

Myrtle turned her head slowly back toward Harbal with a very threatening look in her eyes. He knew that look now; his insides started to gel. "Don't you move one inch," she said, climbing out of the truck, keys in hand, stiletto up her sleeve. Harbal hunkered down into the stiff springs of the seat, trying to keep as much metal between him and that stiletto as possible. Myrtle walked into the showroom, which was a converted garage. The walls were plastered with faded automobile ads, none of which resembled the collection of rotting car carcasses scattered about a crumbling macadam lot. In three minutes, a salesmen dressed in blue plaid pants and wearing a comb-over of twelve hairs that started at his jawline and ended at his left ear approached Myrtle with a toothy smile with several of those toothy's missing.

"Hi, I'm Alvin, and how are you this fine bright morning?"

"I need a car," Myrtle replied, "and I will pay cash for it."

"Well then," Alvin said, "what sort of vehicle are you interested in, we carry a full line of sedans in many makes and models, as well as vans and pickup trucks. I assume you are going to trade in your current vehicle?" He said, with a gleam in his bloodshot eyes.

"I will take that Ford Galaxy 500 you have on your lot," Myrtle replied.

"Excellent!" the Salesman said, "I will grab the keys, find the price, and meet you at the desk."

He walked off, trying not to skip in his excitement and to appear casual as though people bought cars from him all day long. Myrtle looked around the garage showroom filled with dust, cobwebs, and rusty car parts and smiled to herself. She walked up front to where a large rusting metal desk faced toward the parking lot so that the salesman could watch the lot for all those excited buyers and she sat in the folding chair at the front of the desk her back to the window. The Salesman took his seat ceremoniously at the desk facing out the window.

"So, you said this would be paid in cash, correct?" He asked with a huge smile vacant in many locations where proud teeth once stood.

"Price?" Myrtle tilted her head.

"Oh, that car is going for $1,200.00," he replied.

"Fine," said Myrtle, do you need the title to my truck?

There was a pause in the negotiations at this point as Alvin stared out the front window and asked:

"Ah,"... why is your friend running across the desert?" He asked.

Myrtle didn't turn around but replied, "Oh, that's my son, he's an athlete. He's going to meet me in Amarillo."

The man blinked.

"That's two hundred miles from here." He said.

Myrtle smiled, "Yeah, he's fine, he needs exercise. Do you want to sell me a car or do I just take one and leave?" The man looked at her holding out a large wad of bills. She handed him $1,500, which was $300 more than the 1980 lavender Ford Galaxy 500 car was worth, and still watching out the front window, Alvin absently handed her the keys. Myrtle left the showroom, climbed into the driver's seat, and casually drove off the lot. She took a sharp turn off the highway into the desert and followed the dust motes that Harbal was kicking up as he ran. In a couple of minutes, she caught up to him. He started screaming and running faster. She pulled beside him with her window down, hung an elbow out, and kept pace.

"Son," she shouted, "There ain't nothing out here for two hundred miles but sun and dirt and snakes. You sure you want to run all the way through the state cause I ain't gonna go away. You and I got some business to settle and it ain't gonna be over till I say so."

The car stayed right beside Harbal, gradually slowing until he dropped. Then Myrtle got out, picked him up off the ground as he panted in exhaustion, and threw him back into the trunk.

"You been out of the trunk too long she muttered, shaking her head as she poured a bottle of water over him and slammed the lid. Myrtle drove back to the highway, opened a Pepsi, and turned on the radio. In another couple of hours, she opened the trunk and handed Harbal a Pepsi of his own. He took it and said, "Thank you." She slammed the lid. They arrived in Amarillo by nightfall, and Myrtle just drove right through. She wanted to get Harbal to where he was going before anything actually killed him. She pulled out her map and found the next small town of Umbrage, the home of the Buffalo Lake National Wildlife Preserve. There would be a campground there. She arrived at the KOA campground at 9 PM and again asked at the front desk for the most remote site they had. They gave her one right out on the prairie. She drove the Ford Galaxy out to the site and set up her tent before she opened the trunk to let Harbal out. He climbed out of the trunk sweaty, and stiffly sat down on a rock by the fire. Myrtle handed him a plate of beans, some sourdough bread, and beef jerky, the perfect prairie meal. They ate in silence. After the food was gone and the scraps cleaned up, Harbal asked Myrtle what her name was.

"You know my name, you idiot." She said as she rinsed the pans. It's Myrtle, I told you when you arrived, and I told you at the beginning of this trip."

Harbal stared at her. "I want to know your full name," he said.

"You don't need that information," she replied.

"Why won't you tell me your full name?" He repeated.

"What do you need my full name for? You are planning on marrying me?"

Harbal shuddered and kicked a rock into the fire.

"I just figured that since I've been kidnapped an all, I might need that information to give the police when this is over." Harbal added smugly.

"Well, I am not at liberty to reveal that information to you at this time because it is none of your damn business. So set yourself up a sleeping matte and shut up about what doesn't concern you.

Myrtle said and tossed Harbal a blanket. Harbal shook his head and said,

"Thank you." he climbed to his feet and found a suitable spot as far away from Myrtle as he could go without raising questions or falling off the edge of the earth.

Myrtle allowed him to sleep outside on the ground that night, knowing there was nowhere to go and no trouble to find. After a couple of gin and tonics, Myrtle was off to her sleeping bag. She had given Harbal two blankets. He was coming up in the world. Along about 4 AM, Harbal woke. He sensed that something was moving around near their camp. He rolled over on one side to look around but saw nothing. He fell back to sleep. A few minutes later, he heard the noise again and woke up. This time he got up and walked around the camp to relieve himself and try to see what was making the noise. A baby bison, as cute as a button, stepped out of the brushes in front of him. Harbal, having grown up with large animals, thought nothing of this. He simply reached out his hand and petted the little fella on the head like a dog. But growing up in a circus meant no babies, only grown animal performers. So, he did not realize that Momma would not take kindly to some human touching the head of her youngster.

Harbal heard a snort and felt the ground rumble under his feet. In the moonlit distance, he realized that one of the masses he had taken for a mountain was moving. It was growing larger as he watched. Harbal stumbled backward when he realized what it was. The mountain was pounding the ground hard enough to shake the car, and that angry mass was aimed directly at him. He turned and ran like the wind for the open trunk. He cleared the car's rear in one adrenalin-fueled leap and slammed the trunk lid on his way inside. He heard the lid shut, and just as the latch caught, the mamma buffalo rammed straight into the trunk. Her head was the size of a Volkswagen. The car flew forward ten feet, and the sound of the collision brought Myrtle out of her sleeping bag wielding her knife and screaming,

"I'LL KILL THE LOT OF YOU **!!!!!!"

When Myrtle burst from her tent screaming threats and wielding a weapon, the Buffalo turned, saw her, and charged. Myrtle stepped expertly to the side and kicked the animal as it passed. It spun around and charged her again, and again Myrtle sidestepped the beast, only this time she landed a blow to the Buffalo's shoulder with her knife. The beast bucked, screamed, and ran toward the baby, who joined it in a hasty retreat back to the desert. Myrtle bent over with her hands on her knees to catch her breath and then walked to the car and looked at the trunk. "You in there?"

"Yep" was the answer.

"You dead?"

"You're not that lucky," came the muffled voice from inside.

"Always a day late and a dollar short, ain't ya" Myrtle said and then added,

"Well, looks like you're gonna be in there for the rest of the trip because the latch is jammed, and the trunk is caved in.".

"You don't say," was the reply.

"What were you doing outside chasing the buffalos?" Myrtle asked.

"What's your last name," Was Harbal's reply.

"You're a smart ass, you know that?" Myrtle shouted at the dented trunk.

"Thank you," was the reply.

" Well, now that you've managed to piss off the only neighbors, we had within a six-hundred-mile radius there's not much point in staying here any longer, That Buffalo will be back, and she'll probably bring family." she yelled at the dented trunk.

Myrtle gathered her sleeping bag and loose items, throwing them into the car's back seat and sat down to smoke a cigarette. This was one hell of a fix. They still had several days of travel ahead of them and there was no way the boy would survive that long in a hot car trunk. Myrtle would have to drive straight through to Arizona without stopping and even at that, it would be tricky. She couldn’t even douse him with water or throw crackers at him. She climbed into the car, turned the key and started the engine. She sighed at the idea of this long long haul into the jaws of hell, pressed the gas pedal and drove back to the highway toward Albuquerque, still several hundred miles away and there was little to nothing between here and there.

15) Life In An Easybake Oven.

Myrtle pulled off the highway at daybreak and tried to open the trunk again. "You still alive in there?" She asked.

"Yes, thank you," was the muffled reply.

Myrtle wanted to reach Albuquerque, New Mexico, by tomorrow, but the idiot in the trunk would need some fresh air and water before then. In her mind, she mused over people writhing in agony in a sea of lava, and they all looked like Harbal. The image made her sad and happy at once. Still driving west, she got an idea. she took the first ramp off the highway and found a motel. All the gas stations were convenience stores and had no equipment to help her pry open the trunk, but motels had maintenance. She parked the car in front of the check-in window, climbed out, walked inside, and asked the clerk if any garages were nearby. The answer was no. So, she asked them if they could loan her a hand drill for about five minutes. The clerk shrugged her shoulders and called the Manager, who called maintenance, who arrived in about ten minutes with a hand drill.

"Thank you," Myrtle said. "Do you have a 1-inch drill bit?" The maintenance man returned to his toolbox with the size bit she had requested. Myrtle thanked him again and walked outside to the Ford Galaxy, where she said to the trunk, " Where's your head?"

"On my shoulders," Harbal replied.

"Close enough," said Myrtle.

she set the drill on the trunk lid and began drilling air holes. The maintenance man and girl at the front desk watched Myrtle drill holes in the caved-in lid of the trunk. When they heard screaming, the girl called the Manager. By the time the Manager arrived, Myrtle had fully ventilated the trunk. The drill came out a teensey bit red from time to time as the silly crybaby in the trunk was kicking and shrieking but all in all, with the coming heat of the day, she considered her work an act of mercy. "THAT BETTER?" She yelled at the trunk lid. There was a pause before she heard a reluctant "Thank you."

"You're welcome," she said as the Manager trotted outside to ask her what she was doing. He made it about three feet when Myrtle aimed the drill at him and said, "Don't come any closer or I'll shoot." she squeezed the trigger several times to rev the drill. Much to her amazement (even at this point in her colorful life), the Manager raised his hands and backed away.

"Back inside, where you were minding your own business," Myrtle said., The Manager nodded, hands in the air, and carefully backed into the office. Myrtle walked in front of him, drill poised. Once inside, she handed the drill back to the maintenance man, walked out of the office, climbed into the ventilated car, and casually drove off.

At the front counter of the Motel the manager said,"Man, that was a close call," Both the clerk and the Maintenance man stared at him. He shook his head and went back into his office. Harbal, sprouting many perfectly round red holes all over his arms and legs, could see the sky, and the fresh air was welcomed. In another two hours on the road, Myrtle pulled over, got something from the cooler, and walked around to the trunk. "You thirsty?" she asked.

"Yeah," Harbal replied.

"Pick a hole," she said. Harbal's fingertip protruded from a hole on the left side. Passing cars slowed to a crawl as Myrtle began to pour bottled water into the holes in her trunk. When she felt the cars slow down, she glared at them, and they sped off. After the water, Myrtle shoved a couple of String-Cheeses through the holes to the guest inside, climbed back in the car, and drove off. She had to reach Albuquerque before the auto repair shops closed, and Harbal cooked in the heat. She stopped and poured cold water into the designated hole every thirty miles. Harbal said, "Thank you,"

From inside the trunk, Harbal's world had shrunk to a dark, cramped space glittering with holes filled with hot blue sky. His world was focusing for the first time since he fled the circus. He was spending a lot of time in reflection now. He had always had choices; he just kept avoiding the right ones. He was in this trunk by his own doing. He began to self-examine to discover where it had all gone wrong and realized that he could have become a decent 'catcher' and maybe should have stayed with his profession. Maybe he had not thought things through when he fled the Big Top. He began to think about the thrill of it all, seeing his mother in her tight leotards and pink feathers gliding toward him through the air above the gasping crowds, arms outstretched, never for a second doubting his ability to be there with a strong, precise grip, even at the age of ten. Simply not dropping his mother gave him a sort of affirmation that negated all the negative perceptions he had felt surrounding him. But in the civilian world, all he found was jail. He had no idea what would happen next, but he was pretty sure that this was his last trip in the trunk. He knew that he would have expired from the heat by the time Myrtle found a way to free him (if she even wanted to, which she did for some reason).

Harbal Person's life was passing before his eyes, and the only bright spot in it had been the little girl who shared his loneliness for short stops along the way. Harbal closed his eyes and slept. He wanted to die dreaming of her hand holding his. The car vibrated and bumpity bumpity bumpity in a soothing rhythm along the stark highway. The heat in the trunk was rising despite the numerous holes, and Myrtle had the gas pedal indented into the floor. The car shot down straight flat roads under the unbearable weight of the New Mexico sun. Heat waves swam up from the tarmac, and in the distance, the hills danced in the wavering heat. The inside of the car was blistering hot even for Myrtle, who Harbal was sure had been born and raised in Hell. In the trunk, Harbal closed his eyes and said a prayer for the first time in his life. His prayer was simple "If you're listening up there in your cushy clouds, I'd like to ask a favor even though I don't deserve an answer. I'd like this crazy old woman to actually get me to where she is taking me before I cook, so I can at least find out what this has all been about. It wasn't her catching me stealing; we are way beyond THAT. So, if you wouldn't mind, could you please get this over with."

Myrtle was doing the same thing in the front seat. She asked God to help her get this man to his final destination before he turned into Beef Wellington. She was on a mission of the utmost importance unbeknownst to Harbal; since acrobats have nine lives like cats, it was a mission to save what was left of his lives, not just the ones he was now using up in the hot trunk.

16) Outta Control

Myrtle had poured all their drinking water over the trunk to keep Harbal alive. He was becoming bleary and less responsive. She reached Albuquerque at 10 PM, and nothing was open. With the sun gone from the sky she decided to drive straight through. It was the only thing to do. The landscape cooled down rapidly once the sun had set, cooling Harbal with it. He had gone from boiling to shivering in less than two hours. So, Myrtle dug in and drove until dawn the next day. She was exhausted. They were still out in the middle of nowhere. She pulled over to the side of the road and pushed more cheese sticks through the holes in the trunk, poured in the last of her water. Harbal spoke to her through the lid.

"Myrtle," he said.

"Yeah," she replied, stuffing the cheese sticks through the holes.

"I'm really sorry I tried to rob you. You're really a good woman. You took me in and gave me a chance, something no one else would do. I appreciate it."

Myrtle stood stock still and listened. Harbal continued.

"Even with all the stuff you've put me though these last couple of weeks, you never left me behind, and you didn't kill me, have me arrested, or just thrown out. For some odd reason you didn't give up on me and walk away like everyone else has done my whole life.

You stuffed me in here because you have a damn good reason for doing all this, and since I'm still alive, I'm willing to find out what that is. And I also believe that whatever you're doing is important enough to you, to risk everything to do it. I have come to the conclusion, that depending on how you choose to look at the things, either you see things as being done TO you, or being done FOR you, even the bad things, maybe even especially them. So, thank you for whatever is going on, cause I'm aware that I ain't looking at life the same way I used to" He finished.

Myrtle stood outside the trunk fighting back the tears welling in her eyes. It had been a pretty rough trip for the pair of them. She was exhausted, but she was still Myrtle. She cleared her throat.

"Well, we ain't there yet.... but you're welcome," she mumbled.

Myrtle climbed back behind the wheel, pulled out a bag of coffee beans from her stores in the back seat, and chewed the beans. It gave her enough energy to drive for two more hours in the rising heat. At around 10 AM, with the sun beating down on the pair of them, Myrtle fell asleep and ran the car off the road and out into the flatlands where it kept rolling slowly with the weight of Myrtle's sleeping foot pressed lightly on the gas. Eventually, she readjusted herself and let off the gas. The car drifted to a slow stop. Harbal, bleary and beginning to hallucinate about elephants, knew something was wrong as the bouncing of the car gently halted. He began to shout from the trunk and panic when there was no sharp reply. He could not kick like Myrtle could because he was too big, and the trunk lid was mashed against him. The car sat in the middle of the burning desert for two hours with Myrtle asleep against the wheel. The sun had risen to its zenith in the sky above the car.

Harbal found it harder to breathe and nearly impossible to distinguish reality from hallucinations. He was annoyed at the Reindeer dressed in formal wear who obscured his view of the pig roast taking place on the roof of the car. He kept shouting for Myrtle to get in line at the buffet, but she was not answering.

"Please God, you can kill me after I see what is at the end of this @#$%%# rainbow" was the only coherent sentence he had uttered since morning. At around 3 PM, Harbal began the descend into a coma.

One small cloud appeared in the distance of the flat blank desert sky. Then another and another and another. People came out of their homes to see this anomaly. Two clouds formed on the distant horizon; one type was fluffy and playful, and the others were thin and sharp. The two groups of clouds slowly moved across the sky toward the mountains just a mile behind where the car sat. The clouds were keeping pace with each other side by side. Harbal roused himself for the fourth time, watching them through the holes with nearly comatose eyes. In ten minutes, the clouds reached the area about five miles outside Flagstaff and pushed up against the mountains behind the car. When they hit the mountains, they were pushed into each other, and within five minutes, the thin sharp clouds had sliced off the bottom of the big fluffy clouds, and something miraculous happened.

Harbal, now barely clinging to consciousness, heard a loud clap of thunder.

The sky darkened, and it began to rain. Harbal felt the drops of cold water on his arm and side and then on his face. It almost sizzled when it hit him. He turned his head sideways and caught the drops on his tongue. Once his mouth was moist enough to work, he shouted, "THANK YOU!" This time, the rain and his shout woke Myrtle. She raised her head and blinked her eyes. "Oh My God, it's raining," she said out loud. Still moving in thick exhaustion, she opened her door to the downpour and stepped out. "Harbal, you still alive?" She shouted.

"Yeah," was the reply, "but I think the trunk is filling up with water."

"Whine whine whine," Myrtle said. "One minute you're hot, the next minute you're drowning. This ain't no five-star hotel." Harbal smiled. ... She was back.

"Boy, I gotta sleep," she added. "I can't drive no more I am just spent. You ain't gonna drown, there are holes to let the water out. I'll see you in a few, after I get some shut eye."

Myrtle stalked back to the driver's side, climbed in, and laid down across the seats to sleep. The sound of the rain steadily tapping on the roof was a soothing lullaby that carried her to another realm. Harbal did the same. He just arranged a couple of wrenches under his head to keep it up out of the water and relaxed in the cool wet. So, both exhausted souls immersed themselves in the comforts at hand and drifted off to sleep.

17) Prayer Works In Stange And Wonderful Ways

Meanwhile, the water from this rainstorm was accumulating in puddles, crevasses, and crannies of rock, overflowing their tiny banks in the mountains just behind the car, then joining other runnels as they traveled south down the sides of the mountains. Along the way, they swept the hillsides clean of dead wood, soda cans, brush, bottles, old coolers, tires, tent poles, shoes, plastic bags, water bottles, candy wrappers, old film containers, underwear, sleeping bags well; you get the idea. An abandoned city of moving debris like lava was roiling and wending its way down the mountains and into the washes crisscrossing the plains. The gentle rocking of the car soothed Myrtle, who rolled over on her side and snuggled down into the seats. Myrtle was blessed with the rare ability to sleep on the edge of a picket fence. The drumming rain and the gentle rocking were narcotics to the exhausted, as Myrtle and Harbal snoozed. Something large bumped the car. The car jarred and woke Myrtle, who was annoyed at the intrusion. She rolled over on her back, looked up at the car roof, and saw flickering shadows dancing across the lining. It looked for all the world like the reflections of water. So, Myrtle yawning, gripped the wheel and sat up to look at the desert landscape. Her eyes flew open. There was no landscape. It was an expansive seascape, and they were caught on a pile of debris in the middle of a slow-moving ocean. The bump that woke her occurred when a tree trunk rolled under the back tires and came up under the car. There were a couple of smaller trees stuck under the car too. She could see them when she rolled down the window and hung out to look around. They were wedged on a sort of raft made of accumulated debris, and they were moving. It was slow, but they were definitely moving.

Myrtle shouted back to Harbal, 'You awake in there?"

"I am now," Harbal answered. "Are we there yet?" He added.

Myrtle grimaced.

"WHERE DO RIVERS IN DESERTS GO?" Myrtle yelled at the trunk. Harbal barely heard her over the rain; he, too, had noticed the gentle rocking of the car but thought Myrtle was driving again.

"AREN'T YOU DRIVING?" Harbal yelled back over the din of rain on the lid.

"NO, WE ARE FLOATING," she yelled back.

"Floating?" Harbal asked himself out loud. He wiggled his face close to the holes to get lookout with one eye. All he saw was muddy water, moving muddy water. "WHERE'S THE DESERT?" He yelled in alarm.

"UNDER THE WATER!" Myrtle replied.

Harbal yelled, "WHERE DOES ALL THE WATER END UP?"

Myrtle did not reply immediately; she was back inside, scouring her road maps, frantically flipping through the map from page to page. The topography of the area was in colors indicating the rise and fall of the landscape. She did not know exactly where she had run off the road and kept driving after she fell asleep behind the wheel. But she figured they were somewhere above Flagstaff in an area that indicated some rough terrain ahead.

Myrtle's eyes grew to the size of manhole covers. She slammed the map shut on the seat and climbed halfway out the window. "WE GOT US A SITUATION HERE!" she yelled over the rain.

Harbal replied, "THANK YOU."

Myrtle pulled her body back in from the window, cursing under her breath that she had EVER taught that imbecile good manners. She grabbed the map again. The Grand Canyon: They were being swept toward the Grand Canyon.

From the trunk, where Harbal was lying in ten inches of water, he yelled, "HEY, COME ON IN...THE WATER'S FINE."

"SHUT UP OR I WILL STAB YOU THROUGH THE HOLES." she yelled back.

"THANK YOU" was the reply.

Myrtle balled up her fists and beat dents in the dashboard. "Why did I not kill him while I had the chance?" she said through gritted teeth. The car bumped into another log. From the trunk, Harbal shouted,

"CAN WE STOP AND SEE THE GRAND CANYON WHILE WE'RE HERE?" Myrtle gripped the steering wheel in both hands and took several deep breaths to steady herself,

"YOU BET," she replied.

"When will we get there?" Harbal asked.

"IN ABOUT TWENTY MINUTS I FIGURE" Myrtle shouted, "AND WE'RE GOING IN BY THIS RIVER WE'RE FLOATING IN RIGHT NOW" She screamed.

Harbal didn't answer.

Then he shouted, "IS THIS RIVER ENTERING THE GRAND CANYON FROM THE BOTTOM OR THE TOP?"

This time Myrtle didn't answer. She beat dents in the dashboard again.

"I DON'T KNOW WHERE WE ARE," she eventually shouted back through gritted teeth.

After a short pause, Harbal replied:

"WE ARE IN A FLOOD, IN THE MIDDLE OF A DESERT, IN A PURPLE FORD GALAXY 500. DOES THAT HELP?"

Myrtle lost her temper. She rolled her window down, climbed through it to the car's roof, stalked back to the trunk, and started staving it in further with one foot. Harbal was screaming “STOP IT #$%^%# YOU’RE BLOCKING MY VIEW OF THE OCEAN‼” Myrtle stopped and stood on the floating car studying the landscape. Ah, seascape. The mountains on the other side were coming closer by the minute, and according to the map, so were some "variations in topography," which meant depressions in the ground, which is a less threatening description than saying a one mile drop into the gaping maws of the Grand Canyon in a car with a smart-ass lunatic in the trunk.

Myrtle looked down at glimpses of Harbal through the holes in the lid. Then she just sat down.

"What are you doing?" Harbal asked, looking up at Myrtle's backside through the holes.

"I am contemplating our future," Myrtle replied.

"What future?" Harbal said.

"Exactly," Myrtle muttered.

"Have you tried speaking to a pastor?" Harbal asked.

"I'm going to kill you," she hissed

"Thank you," he replied.

Myrtle stood up and started stomping the trunk again.

18) Old Acrobats Never Die

All the debris caught under and around the car created a floating island that moved more slowly than the water around it. More thunder rumbled in the distance as jagged streaks of white and blue lightning shot horizontally across the darkened sky. The storm was coming their way. The rain grew heavier, and the sky turned to a blue-black bruise. Another log hit the car island and spun it slowly around and around as it drifted toward its Fate. Myrtle sat on the roof and watched the scene unfold dismally detached. Up a creek without a paddle played in a loop in her mind. Harbal watched her on the roof. It began to unnerve him to see Myrtle so defeated. At no time during their little outing did she give him the impression that she was not always six steps ahead of anything in her path. It was so unlike her. A gin bottle floated up beside Harbal. He got an idea and opened the bottle. "Hey, Myrtle, I have some gin here, wanna smell the cap?" Myrtle began cursing and stomping the trunk with her heels. Harbal took his first-ever sip of gin and immediately spit it out in a fine mist through one of the holes in the trunk lid. Myrtle, now in a rage, stood up and started to jump up and down on the trunk lid in angry frustration at her inability to murder him, and suddenly, to their mutual amazement, the lid popped. It raised about three inches and bounced up and down.

Myrtle scurried back to the roof to allow it to open. Harbal carefully pushed the lid all the way open and slowly stood up.

"THANK YOU," he shouted to the sky, receiving a mouthful of rain. "But I was comfortable where I was. We're going over a falls if you wanna watch," he muttered at the sky as he glanced at Myrtle through the holes in the standing lid. Her arms were folded, her face resigned. They were surrounded by debris, mud, and hopelessness, like Harbal's life in general. So, he just shrugged and sat back in the trunk to watch the last chapter of his life bump and swirl its way to its conclusion. Myrtle moved to the hood to watch as uprooted trees floated past them. In a few more minutes, the roar of a falls began to grow louder than the rain on the hood, and Myrtle noticed things disappearing from the landscape in the distance. They had reached the first 'variation in the landscape,' a chasm and the falls. Harbal heard it, too, and could see from Myrtle's posture that it was coming fast. As they closed the distance, Myrtle could see many large tree snags building up at the edge of the falls and knew that the chasm was not wide. Maybe the car island would catch in the build-up and stop there, but she was a practical woman and knew their odds were slim. The car island began to spin slowly, and Harbal saw the edge coming up. He had another idea based on a hunch he had been formulating.

He stood up. "Myrtle," he yelled over the roar of the falls and the driving rain, "LOOK SHARP, THIS CAR IS GOING TO FALL OUT FROM UNDER US."

Myrtle swung around, looked at him, and yelled, "YOU DON'T SAY"...then understanding hit her. She spun around to see the massive deadfalls wedged across the chasm. The car began spinning faster as the loose debris hit it from behind. If the colliding debris did not take the deadfalls down with it over the falls, then the deadfalls would be sturdy enough to provide them handholds. Myrtle and Harbal stared at each other. They spoke the same language as Harbal had come to suspect. The car island bumped trees and spun, bumped more trees, and suddenly the tree trunks beneath the car tipped over the edge, and Harbal and Myrtle both saw the depth of the chasm. Myrtle scrambled back to the trunk near Harbal, who had climbed out and stood on the lid. Harbal, looking at Myrtle, shouted for her to grab a branch when the car tipped. She gave the nod and focused on the highest branch she could reach. Harbal figured the car would upend itself, giving them both the height they needed to reach the higher limbs and would then drop out from beneath them; at least they would not go over the falls with it. They may outlast the flood and climb back to solid ground if they could hold on well enough. The purple Ford Galaxy 500 rose beneath them like a dying whale broaching the ocean's surface one last time. Then, as the trees pushed the car over the ledge in a grinding roar, Myrtle leaped into the air on Jackhammer legs and grabbed the limb she had scoped out as they approached. Harbal caught a root with one hand about thirty feet below Myrtle. They both hung there watching in rapt fascination as the old For Galaxy 500 slammed back and forth against the chasm's walls. The seats dropped out, the toolbox, and two bottles of gin. Then the cooler followed it into the roiling abyss below. Harbal reached another handhold and climbed up from the root to stand on the trunk wedged across the chasm. He looked up at Myrtle. She was hanging comfortably from a thick limb above his head and looking down at him. She had a look in her eyes he had never seen on any face in his life. Myrtle looked down at Harbal with a deep emotion that seemed out of place under their current circumstances.

Myrtle was looking down at Harbal with tears in her eyes. She was doing this for her niece, whom she loved more than her own life. After Harbal fled the circus, the girl searched for Harbal for years. She was still searching, and Myrtle knew she would never stop. So, Fate brought a broken Harbal to Myrtle's doorstep, and, like it or not, their fates were forever intertwined. She was willing to go over the falls with him. She would not be able to face her niece otherwise. It seemed a fitting end. So, Myrtle hanging from a limb a hundred of feet above a raging chasm, relaxed and smiled at Harbal. No matter where life had taken her, she was circus to the core.

Harbal being Harbal, chose this time to ask his real question, the question that had bothered him since the night he watched Myrtle wrap her legs around a pine tree and shinny up to tie off an overhead line. It was a move commonly used by professional riggers in circuses; it was a skill taught to children as soon as their legs were long enough to lock around a pole. So, since this was their existential moment, Harbal called up to Myrtle from his position on the trunk.

"HEY, MYRTLE, WHAT DID YOU SAY YOUR LAST NAME WAS?" He shouted.

"I AM NOT IN A POSITION TO REVEAL THAT INFORMATION AT THIS TIME," was her reply.

"WELL, MYRTLE, IT SEEMS TO ME THAT THE POSITION YOU ARE IN, RENDERS ANY PREVIOUS AGREEMENTS NULL AND VOID, AND SINCE WE ARE BOTH ABOUT TO PLUMMET TO OUR DEATHS, DON'T YOU THINK YOU OWE ME A LITTLE BIT OF CLOSURE?" Harbal shouted back.

Myrtle paused.

"MY LAST NAME IS... Ashton," Myrtle shouted back.

"Really," Harbal uttered to himself. He knew the name, and although they were an excellent high-wire act, they were mostly clowns. He thought for a second" "WHAT WAS YOUR MAIDEN NAME THEN?" He shouted. There was a long silence this time as they both hung over the chasm amidst the boiling debris, but finally she answered:

“My maiden name was "Wallenda." She said.

The name hit Harbal so hard it nearly knocked him off the tree. He had suspected she was circus, but this? This was a whole different level of shock. The Wallenda was likely the finest and most famous high-wire family in circus history. It was rumored they could do anything as long as it was in mid-air. Harbal was speechless. He felt his throat catch as he stared up in awe at Myrtle Wallenda Ashton, almost a God, once known as ‘The Iron Butterfly’’ a legend spoken only with the utmost of reverence for her strength and courage, to every child born in the circus. The Iron Butterfly, who saved three members of her family in a deadly accident in Canada where they were performing the only act of its kind in the world, “the Seven people pyramid,” when the cable slipped causing the pyramid to collapse. Myrtle fell from the top, landed midsection on the cable breaking four ribs, and grabbed family members as they dropped past her. One after another fell and caught tight to Myrtle. Myrtle held them hanging from her arms and legs for twenty minutes while nets were pulled into place. She sustained four broken ribs, two dislocated shoulders, one torn rotator, and ACL tears in both knees. She did not once whimper but kept reassuring her family as they hung from her breaking body, that they would be fine. Myrtle's husband, father, and one sister died in the accident, and Myrtle left the circus. Later she would be recognized by the industry as the greatest 'sky-walker' in circus history. Harbal stared up at her. Any anger, or animosity he held toward her evaporated in the explosion of awe that washed him clean.

Harbal shouted up to Myrtle, "BEFORE THIS TREE FALLS, TELL ME WHY YOU DRAGGED ME ON THIS MISERABLE TRIP INSTEAD OF LOCKING ME UP."

There was more silence, and then "BECAUSE MY NIECE IS LOOKING FOR YOU. SHE'S BEEN SEARCHING FOR TEN YEARS. I FOUND YOU BY ACCIDENT AND AM TAKING YOU BACK TO HER SO SHE CAN SEE WHAT AN ASSHOLE YOU ARE AND GET OVER HER CRUSH."

Harbal who was still in shock at whom his captor had been, was once again struck with another bolt of emotional lightening. A new sense of urgency filled him matching the lightning bolts crackling over their heads. Myrtle continued,

"SHE USED TO SNEAK OUT TO VISIT YOU WHEN OUR CIRCUSES PASSED BY...SHE GOT HER ASS WHIPPED EVERY TIME. SHE STILL DID IT. I FIGURED IT WAS TIME TO PUT THIS SITUATION TO REST." Myrtle finished.

Harbal was shaken and unable to answer as he stood there, his emotions swirling in hundreds of directions.

Myrtle watched the impact of this revelation as it hit Harbal. She saw all of it in his bright glistening eyes; eyes that not long ago were dead with defeat. Then she shouted,

"DO YOU THINK THERE ARE ALLIGATORS IN THAT RIVER BELOW?"

Harbal, hearing these words, snapped out of his shock. A broad, genuine smile spread across his face, rivaling the sun that would soon break across the horizon after the storm passed. He choked back a couple of tears, looked up at Myrtle hanging from the branch, and yelled, "YES, CROCODILES, ALLIGATORS, GIANT SQUID, AND IN YOUR CASE...DINOSAURS."

"I'M GONNA STAB YOU ONCE I GET JOANNA'S PERMISSION." Replied Myrtle.

Harbal immediately studied the catch zone around him, doing a well-honed visual measure of the direction, distance, aerial disturbances like wind, rain, falling trees and speed at which, she would arrive. Then he shouted to Myrtle: "SWING AND DO A 1/4 TWIST THROW YOUR HIPS LEFT TWO FEET, ARMS-OUT-CATCH FOR SAFETY.... I WILL CATCH YOU."

Now, Myrtle was the one smiling. "I know you will," she said under her breath with an enormous smile.

19) Finding Home

Myrtle focused. The driving rain, the roar of the waterfall, and the crackling of lightning faded from her ears. She looked down and saw her target. This was a one-shot deal, but then this was always a one-shot deal in this line of work. She calculated the drop zone, speed, and differential where she hung, and Harbal stood. She factored in the information Harbal had shouting up to her. When both of their calculations matched, she nodded to Harbal. The river was several hundred feet below and boiling with every sort of trash imaginable, including her car and, of course, the 'alligators,' that old circus jokes well known to high-wire acts. Her target was standing on a log, wedged between the ravine's sides, thirty feet down, ten feet out. Piece of cake, she thought. Of course, this would have been a lot easier twenty years ago, but she was still in shape. She only wore those giant Muumuus because she ran an all-male boarding house. Myrtle, at the age of 42, with gray streaks in her jet-black hair, had not lost her trim and wore the loose ugly clothing to make sure she never had to defend it. And now, the Iron Butterfly hanging from a tree limb poised over the side of the Grand Canyon began to swing expertly back and forth on the limb to build the momentum she would need to throw her body precisely ten feet out over the raging ravine in Harbal's direction from a thirty-foot drop. When she had reached the right degree of swing, she let go of the limb, did a one-quarter turn in midair facing her catcher, and threw her hips to the left, which moved her body directly over Harbal. She held her arms out at 90-degree angles from her body, a position known as the 'safety catch' and dropped toward Harbal at roughly thirty miles per hour. He caught her under the arms absorbing her weight with slightly bended knees, for Myrtle, it was like he was standing on cement, then, in one fluid movement, he gently sat her down on the trunk next to him, took her hand and took a bow for the audience of roaring water, broken cars, and of course, the alligators and in her case dinosaurs. It was a routine they had both cut their teeth on twenty-five years apart, in different lives, with different partners, but it was still the same gig.

"I know who you are," Harbal said., "You were billed as the 'Iron Butterfly."

Myrtle smiled and said, "I'm still going to stab you in the eye when my niece throws you over for an affair with a Bagpipe."

Both grinning, they turned to start the climb up the tree trunk wedged across the ravine to the solid ground. They reached a small plateau, which was a spit of land broken off from the chasm itself, like the center of an M. The water was rushing over both sides of the outside walls. They crawled and pushed their way through more branches as they closed the distance between them and the spit of land. The rain beat down around them like tiny explosions on the hard wet ground. The flood of debris behind them took turns hurling itself over the side of this small canyon in the frenzied white water. Another large log, rolling over and over in the violent waters struck the tree they were using as their bridge and dislodged it from the wall. They felt it jar and tremble as the ground beneath the rootball dissolved in the torrent of water. The tree began to upend in preparation to drop. Myrtle was closest to the head of the tree that was now a turning network of limbs. They knew they were lost as the mesh of branches they clung to began sliding down the canyon wall toward the boiling water below. It was their good fortune that there were rock outcrops at 45degree angles on the sides of canyons. Harbal screamed at Myrtle to jump. She heard him as the sound of roaring water consumed his voice. Myrtle saw the outcrops rising up beneath them, she let go her hold on the tree and threw herself at the rock. She landed hard but she rolled and was on her feet again immediately. She turned to look back for Harbal who slammed into her chest and knocked them both to the ground. They lay there clutching the rocks and working to calm their breath. The tree grew smaller as it dropped into the frenzied water and disappeared. Neither of them moved, both of them gasping and shaking the water off their heads.

Harbal started looking around for handholds, he saw the slope they were on was at a hard angle and knew they couldn't stay where they were for long. Although the water was rushing into the gorge from behind them, there was no way of knowing when another large object driven over the side by the rushing water would hit the foot of the plateau where they clung. Harbal was on his feet slipping in the scree of small stones that made hill climbing nearly impossible, but the rain had helped to glue the debris in place. Myrtle struggled to her feet as well to examine the environment for handholds, or maybe a taxicab they could hail.

"We have to climb this slope on our hands and knees," Harbal shouted at Myrtle over the noise; then he grimaced and added that his knees were still raw after his adventure with the chair.

Myrtle lowered herself to her knees in the loose gravel. She was very glad of Bertha's blue jeans. She heard Harbal curse as he did the same and tried to push himself up the incline on those raw knees of his. Myrtle stopped crawling and stared at him. He turned to look back at her and when their eyes met, she said,

"You are the biggest crybaby who ever lived."

"I am not" Harbal replied with indignation.

"Yes, you are." Myrtle replied. "You have done nothing but complain since I met you. Oh, my head hurts, oh my ass hurts, oh you're drilling holes in my..." Before she could finish Harbal slid back down beside her, bent forward on his feet. He shoved his hand into the waist of her pants and stood up holding her like a suitcase.

"Put me down you moron!"

Harbal dug his feet into the scree and one terrifying step at a time he walked up the escarpment holding Myrtle by her pants.

They reached the wall of stone on the face of the canyon and Harbal, with a sardonic smile, dropped Myrtle on the ground.

Myrtle laid there looking down at the ground so that Harbal would not see her own sardonic smile. Then she said,

“Well now that you have managed to walk upright for the first time in your miserable life, the first thing you do is walk smack into a wall.”

“Well, that’s life” Harbal replied with a grin. He gained his first handhold of rock and started climbing.

“So, you just gonna leave and old women on a pile of rocks to die then?”

“Yep” was Harbal’s reply.

“First place, I don’t know any old women, and second, the last one to the top is a...”

Myrtle passed him. Harbal laughed out loud as he watched the Iron Butterfly scale the rock wall like she was on flat ground. He joined her in the climb.The mesa was attached at one end, so it was not an island, and the advantage was that the water coming down from the mountains was washing in from two sides and did not reach this spit of land. They both sat down in the rain to wait out the storm. It was the only safe place since the runoff had picked up nearly the entire desert floor and pushed it over the edge. They sat there for a while before Myrtle spoke.

"Why did you leave the circus?" She asked.

Harbal looked at her in wonder, "Because there was an Elephant's ass with my name on it," he replied. Myrtle started laughing. She looked at him in the driving rain, pushing her gray-black hair out of her face, and said,

"You were the best catcher in the business even at ten years old."

Harbal looked at her like she had just told him he was a little headless girl. He shook his head and laughed.

"No, I wasn't, my father was the best catcher in the business."

Myrtle became serious with a dark distant look in her eyes.

"No, he wasn't, Harbal. You were, and your father did everything in his power to keep you out of HIS spotlight. He put you in harm's way at every opportunity. You got the shit jobs, slept with the animals, and took the beatings for your mother."

Harbal sat with his head down, remembering these things like they were yesterday. Yes, his father did glue him to that Elephant; ban him from the family quarters; yes, Harbal often threw himself in front of his mother when his father was drunk and trying to hit her. Yes, every word she said was accurate. After a moment's pause, Myrtle went on,

"We all knew what he was, we all knew what he did, but you know, you can't interfere in another man's family, so we all just watched and swore that if anything ever happened to you, we would throw him under the train. You were a star, Harbal, he was a clumsy drunken hack."

Harbal stood up and walked away from her, hands on his hips. He had left the circus because he believed that he was reviled by them all, and next in line for the Elephant's seat. Now that Myrtle had revealed this different side, things began to shift in his head to make a lot more sense. And then there was the girl. She came despite the retribution she knew she would receive; she always brought kindness and gifts. Her tiny consistent acts of kindness were what had sustained him through one nightmare after another. The rain was letting up and the sky was clearing enough to head for the road. They had to keep moving. Once that sun came back out, they would steam like crabs. And for once, this mattered to Harbal. Suddenly, the life he had lived, which had always been about the past,' had suddenly become a future. He knew who he was now; the confusion was gone. He looked over at Myrtle and smiled,

"We gotta find a road," he said. Myrtle nodded her head yes and stood up soaked through to the skin, she swept her long gray/black hair behind her head and squeeze water out of her T-shirt as she walked. They looked for a direction out of the current desert mud flats. The sun broke through the clouds, and the heat was coming back. In twenty minutes, steam began to rise from the ground, and small creatures skittered over the desert floor and back into the drying burrows for shelter. The pair had no idea how far they were from the highway, so they kept traveling west. It got hotter by the minute until Harbal stopped, bent over, scooped up a handful of mud, and promptly threw it at Myrtle, hitting her squarely in the back.

She spun around, grinning, and said,

"You know, when you showed up on my doorstep, you were as empty as the surface of the moon, just like all the others. You kept repeating the same bad decisions day in and day out. It doesn't look to me like the 'decision' making skills have improved. Myrtle scooped up a handful of mud and hurled it at Harbal's head. He just stood there and let it hit him.

The next ten minutes would cover them both from head to foot with a muddy sunscreen. Still laughing, they hit Route 40 around 6 pm, covered in mud, bleeding in places and both limping. They found a road sign and began to walk back toward Flagstaff. They were both unidentifiably covered in mud, but they made it to the out skirts of Flagstaff alive on foot by 10 PM. Civilization started to appear the closer they got. A few sparse and dilapidated buildings now empty with hollow black windows, stared at them with suspicion as they past. They found a filling station and borrowed their water hose and hosed themselves off, they both finished up in their respective rest rooms, where Myrtle made a call before asking where they could get a hot meal. The attendant told them there was a strip mall up the road about a mile, with a 24hr Waffle House. They looked at each other and laughed. Myrtle was still wearing her Waffle House T-shirt and the jeans Bertha had given her.

They made the trek in good time and without further incident, entered the Waffle House by midnight and slid into a booth in the back. The restaurant was empty except for them. Harbal ordered nearly everything on the menu as Myrtle nodded her approval. The food came hot and steaming and tasted unusually good for some reason, maybe because near death experiences do tend to heighten sensations. Harbal tossed his fork down on the plate just as a lime green Volkswagen Beatle festooned with giant pink flowers similar to the one's on the Muumuu's Myrtle always wore, pulled into the Waffle House parking lot. Myrtle smiled and elbowed Harbal, who was downing his fourth Pepsi. The car's side door opened and out hopped a clown, and then another, and another until a dozen clowns had gathered in the parking lot heading for the door of the Waffle House. Myrtle and Harbal were on their feet. The clowns came in one at a time and hugged Myrtle and shook hands enthusiastically with Harbal, Harbal was speechless as they gripped his arm with affection and staring at him in awe, and then the last clown stepped up to him, and when she took his hand, Harbal was home. He instantly knew her touch, and it felt like no time had passed. It was Joanna. She was all grown up and beautiful. She squeezed Harbal's hand and said softly...

"It's really you," and wrapped her arms around him in a hug that swallowed him whole. He returned the embrace, standing there, circled in cheering clowns. And in this moment saturated in joy, Harbal tore his eyes away from Joanna's to look up at Myrtle and say...

"THANK YOU"

www.ingramcontent.com/pod-product-compliance
Ingram Content Group UK Ltd.
Pitfield, Milton Keynes, MK11 3LW, UK
UKHW021916190726
13853UKWH00002B/695